KY-003-546

Indoor Plants

COLLINS NUTSHELL BOOKS

Indoor Plants

LESLIE JOHNS

With Photographs

COLLINS
LONDON AND GLASGOW

GENERAL EDITOR: J. B. FOREMAN, M.A.

First published 1964

Contents

1

HOUSE PLANTS IN A NUTSHELL

Only a few years ago house plants were grown only by the green-fingered, gardeners with heated greenhouses or the "contemporary" minded. There was a general feeling that they were difficult to grow, rare and expensive, suitable only for modern furnishings and demanding of special conditions in the way of lighting and heating.

To-day there can be few homes in the country without at least one example of a house plant. They have been recognised as simple to grow, decorative and satisfying in a very special kind of way, inexpensive, long lasting, and a splendid means of furnishing an empty corner or a bare wall.

Like so many domestic furnishings (for they can now be accepted more or less in this category), they have developed out of all recognition. Where we can all recognise and accept an ivy, an India rubber plant and perhaps a philodendron, few of us can differentiate between certain nidulariums or aechmeas. And again we may not appreciate that it just doesn't matter whether or not we know the names. It is the decorative function that is important.

House plants to-day are even easier to grow than they were ten years ago. Many of them are cheaper. Most of them are more colourful, more hardy, more tolerant of poor conditions of light and of extremes of cold and warmth. The commercial growers of house plants have had time to seek better varieties from all over the world, to breed new strength and new colour into them, and to produce for our pleasure plants which simply do not need green fingers. Certain minimums of care and attention are all they demand.

In the following pages a number of the most popular, inexpensive and easily raised house plants are described, and brief advice on their general care is given.

Before I define exactly what I mean by a house plant I should, perhaps, give one important word of advice. House plants are nothing to be afraid of. They are no more than a piece of living vegetation which will give great pleasure, but which should really be accepted into the home in much the same way that a bunch of flowers is. House plants cost no more than flowers, but given reasonable care will give many times more value. They should be regarded as expendable, though of course every effort should be made to see that they not only last as long as possible but give good decorative value during this period.

Nearly everything that grows in a garden can, with varying success and varying satisfaction, be grown indoors. The difficulties are practical ones of plant and root size. Most plants will not of course live as long indoors as in garden soil, but they will certainly last as long as cut flowers. If nearly everything in the garden can be grown indoors, how then does one define a house plant? I was once asked to do just this for the purposes of a flower show. To the best of my recollection my definition was as follows.

"Any living plant grown in a pot or other container under normal living conditions in a home because of the beauty of its flower or foliage and its long life in all seasons under these conditions." This definition severely limits us, but it means that we confine ourselves to plants robust or adaptable enough to accept the somewhat artificial conditions of indoor living. Cacti and succulents also fit into this definition, but because they are a law unto themselves (and so demand a book unto themselves) they are not discussed in detail here.

In the old days of the conservatory, many plants could be grown in its light and humid atmosphere which would not take happily to life further inside the home. The conservatory is now a thing of the past, being replaced by the sun lounge, which is almost as good. Its passing, however, inconveniences us little because passed also is the use of domestic gas for lighting. Gas is certainly an enemy of plants and few live happily in a room with a gas fire. The infinitesimal amount of gas that escapes from these appliances, however efficient they may be, is for some reason particularly inimical to plants. Natural gasses, in fact, such as those given off by fruit, are again death both to plants and to cut flowers. No florist-fruiterer will store flowers and fruit together if he knows his job.

I must confess to a preference for foliage rather than flowering plants. This purely personal preference is due partly to my own liking for the greater subtlety of shape, colour and texture obtained from leaves, but it is due also to the knowledge that a flower is a less permanent thing than the leaves which it supplements. Some house plants, such as the delightful Grecian Urn plant or *Aechmea fasciata*, may produce flowers rarely, but the flower lasts for weeks and is followed by the delicate coloured bracts which extend its life even longer.

Fortunately in foliage plants we are presented with a wealth of difference in shape. There is everything from the huge slash leaves of the *Monstera deliciosa* to the spear-like foliage of Mother-in-Law's Tongue or *Sansevieria trifasciata*. In colour, green naturally predominates, but white, gold, silver, scarlet, purple, pink, orange, are all to be seen, particularly in the more "modern" plants. In textures we range from the hard and glossy foliage of the India Rubber Plant, *Ficus elastica*, to the soft and hairy tissue of the Indoor Lime tree, *Sparrmannia africana*, and the spiky glochids of cacti. The range is tremendous and the problem is merely one of choice.

If one is to grow house plants then one must know where to place them. Undoubtedly the best place in the average home is in or near a south or west facing window. This position offers the plant the maximum benefit of plenty of light. Not all plants demand this light, and some will live happily in a comparatively dark corner. We can make a general rule here and say that the darker the green of leaf and the firmer and woodier the texture of the plant, the less light it requires. In general it is true to say that all plants with light coloured foliage or with soft and sappy growth require as much light as they can get, other than direct sunlight burning through the glass of the window.

If plants are placed in a window, although they gain the benefit of good lighting, they suffer the perils of damage from draughts and possibly from frosts in a cold winter. They must receive protection from both. Although no plants like a draught, whether cold or hot, they all like a certain amount of fresh air. An over-heated, stuffy, tobacco-smoke-filled room suits most house plants less than the comparatively cold but cleaner air of a chilly British bedroom or an unheated box-room.

Watering

The main requirements of house plants are those of all living things: some protection from weather, food and water, and a certain basic minimum of cleanliness. Unfortunately, while a human and an animal can refuse an excess of food and drink, a plant can only accept what is given to it, and as a rule house plants are given far too much. The greatest faults in house plant care are overfeeding and over-watering. More plants are killed in particular by being drowned than by any other form of ill-treatment. However, it is quite impossible to lay down hard-and-fast rules about either feeding or watering. Not only do different plants have different requirements, but differences in climate, differences in position in a room, differences of heating systems and their efficiency all make it quite impossible to say that this plant must be watered once a week and that one every day. The main thing to bear in mind always about watering, is that seldom and thoroughly is much to be preferred to little and often. Having learnt the lesson that most house plants die from drowning, many enthusiasts are apt to go to the other extreme and allow their plants to get almost dry, giving them a tiny dribble from the watering-can or kettle. This will wet the surface of the soil in the pot, and it will then appear that the whole of the root ball is moist. Un-fortunately only the top is wet, and the main root system remains starved of moisture, while the wet top is apt to set up rot at the base of the plant stem.

By far the most efficient way of watering house plants is to dip the entire pot into a bucket of water until the water begins to trickle over the top. When air bubbles cease to rise from the soil surface, the entire root system has received as much water as it can take. The plant should then be removed from the water and stood in a safe place, so that all excess moisture can drain away. This second part of the exercise is as important as the first. As water drains from the pot and through the hole in the base, it sucks air into the soil. This air is just as important as the water, and it is the lack of air in over-watered plants that kills them.

In winter, probably the most critical time for watering, it is best to leave most house-plants until they show signs of flagging before they are watered. There are exceptions to this rule. Certain plants such as some of the bromeliads, nidulariums, and other stiff leaved plants such as sansevieria will give little indication of water shortage. One or two plants, such as the zebra plant or aphelandra, and *Ficus pumila*, must never be allowed to dry out. Their root ball must always be kept moist.

More precise indications of water requirements are given in the sections devoted to individual plants.

Feeding

Unless plants are actually in flower or are growing strongly, it is a wise general rule to give no fertiliser of any kind during the winter months, that is between the end of October and the beginning of March. This policy, together with the withholding of significant amounts of water, will help the plants to rest and ripen. Once the days begin to get longer and warmer again, watering should begin to be more frequent, and tiny amounts of fertiliser can be given. There is, I believe, little to choose between the various types of proprietory fertilisers on the market. It is important, however, that they be used strictly according to instruction on the packet or bottle, and that they be used only when the plant can obviously take an additional course of feeding.

Newly potted plants or any with damaged or immature roots can only be harmed when given fertiliser, and an overdose is always dangerous. If plants are brought from a reputable source, they will be potted in a soil mixture which will be sufficient to feed the plant, certainly for the first six to twelve months of its new life in the home. After this date it is helpful to give a modest diluted feed, probably at every alternate watering during the summer months. Liquid feeds are probably the easiest to apply but only a few drops of concentrate should be allowed to each pot. If the pot is dry it should be watered before feeding so that the roots are in a condition to accept the chemicals.

One of the best ways of ensuring that the whole of the root ball of a plant is maintained in a healthy, moist and well-fed condition, is to insert the pot into another larger container with the space between packed with some moisture retentive material such as peat, moss, crumpled Florapak, vermiculite or sand. If this material is kept constantly moist then the pot can absorb that moisture through its base and sides.

Humidity

Keeping the pot in this way inside another moisture retentive container also helps to provide a little humidity to the plant. This humidity is probably the factor of healthy life most missed by all house plants grown in the average home. Many of our house plants come originally from moist and steamy jungles, and they have arrived in the home via the glass-house with its carefully controlled balance of heating and humidity. Human beings tend to heat their homes and maintain them in warm dry conditions that are actively disliked by most plants. Although we attempt to give plants the conditions they require for a healthy life, we obviously cannot and will not do this if it means living ourselves in a steamy, uncomfortable and furniture-damaging atmosphere.

Fortunately, most of the plants we grow in our homes have been bred and conditioned to accept a lesser degree of humidity than they would receive in their natural and original surroundings. We can give them some degree of vapour by allowing water to evaporate from an external container or from gravel-filled trays on which the plants stand. We can also give them an occasional spray with an atomiser, and we can make sure that in times of suitable weather the plants get some access to outdoor air, which is generally more humid than the air inside the house.

The warmth and consequent humidity of air in a home depend on the type and extent of heating, and on the variations in horizontal levels in a room. Warm air rises and consequently air at ceiling level is usually dryer and warmer than by the floor. For this reason it is sometimes unwise to grow plants on tall stands where they will live constantly in the hot dry air near the ceiling. It is also a somewhat hazardous practice to train climbers upwards to the extent that they reach this poor atmosphere. Fortunately here the root ball and the lower leaves will be in the cooler and moister air, but the delicate growing tips will be in grave danger of damage.

During the summer months it is frequently helpful to stand plants out-of-doors, either for a few weeks at a time, depending of course on the type, shape and size of the plant, or merely during a brief warm shower. One of the most attractive of our own plants is an ivy which over 10 years or so has become a lovely climber 8 or 10 feet tall. This grows happily in a static position in our country home, and one of the reasons for its continuing glossy health is, I am sure, that it enjoyed its six months sojourn set in the ground. If the pot is buried in soil it need not be specially watered, and both roots and foliage will enjoy a closer communion with nature than is obtained inside the average home.

This vexed question of humidity is indeed an important point with some of our loveliest house plants. In particular it must be regarded as a matter of real importance so far as the *saintpaulia* or African violet is concerned. Here one is able to indulge these plants occasionally with an atmosphere which they enjoy, and indeed require, by means of a method which though not essential is certainly helpful. The pot containing the saintpaulia or other plant should be placed inside another larger and water-proof container. This in turn is stood inside a much larger bowl or basin. The last is half filled with boiling water, from which the steam escapes to rise up around the plant without the water itself touching it. The moist air in the form of steam is enjoyed by the plant, and indeed adds significantly to the general humidity of the room at large.

A less effective but still useful way of carrying out the same procedure, is to pour hot though not boiling water on to the moisture-retaining material packed between flower pot and exterior containers. Once again a certain amount of steam or water vapour will arise, and although on this occasion hot water will tend to be absorbed through the base and side walls of the flower pot itself, by the time it actually reaches the plant roots, it will be sufficiently cool to do no damage.

Re-potting

Every house plant, if given sufficient care, will one day out-grow the original pot in which it was bought. In this case it must be re-potted into a new container, preferably about one inch wider in diameter than the original. There are two means of discovering whether or not a plant needs re-potting into a larger container. In the first place, it is possible to tell by the retardation of growth that the plant is not developing as it should. If it is receiving normal water and an occasional feed it should be growing upwards and outwards, and if this does not occur then the root system will almost certainly have filled the pot, and ab-sorbed all the nourishment from the soil. Each watering and each feed will then go straight through the pot, with-out providing the hair roots with the moisture and nourish-ment that the plant requires to continue further growth.

A more accurate means of ascertaining whether or not a plant needs re-potting is to knock the plant from its pot and examine the roots visually. This is done by placing the fingers of the hand over the open end of the pot, with the main plant stem between first and second fingers. If the pot is then reversed so that the plant hangs downwards, and its edge is given a sharp knock against any convenient horizontal surface, the pot itself will be projected upwards while the root ball falls out into the hand. If the roots are coiled evenly around the outside of the mass, so that they would in fact run around the walls of the pot, then it is time the plant was re-potted. The procedure then is to slip the plant back into its present pot, and prepare a larger home for it as soon as is convenient.

The new pot as I have said should be at least one inch larger in diameter. If it is an old pot it should be thoroughly cleaned, and if it is a new one it should be soaked some 24 hours in clean water. A crock (a piece of broken flower pot) or a disc of perforated zinc should be placed over the hole at the bottom of the pot to prevent the soil being washed through. A base of new soil (see p. 17) should be placed over this and then the existing root ball should be put in position and held while fresh soil is placed between it and the wall of the pot. This should gradually be added to and firmed in position with the thumbs, until the total of new soil plus the original root ball reaches a level no higher than an inch or so from the top of the pot. The whole surface should then be firmed securely, but not rammed, lest the soil become so compacted that drainage becomes difficult. A final tap or two with the base of the pot on a level surface will secure the old and new soils. A thorough watering will tend to link the old and new soils, and the pot can then be left on one side to drain and to become almost dry until it is watered again.

The object here is to encourage tiny root hairs to grow into the new soil, both to provide the plant with the nourishment it requires, and to blend the new and old soils together, as an eventual home for the plant.

Fatshedera lizei

Anthurium scherzerianum

Philodendron Red Burgundy

Calathea

Anthurium andrianum

Dieffenbachia arvida exotica

Aechmea fasciata

Cissus antarctica

Sometimes the major part of the soil in an old pot will have been used, yet it will not really be necessary to re-pot the plant completely. In this case it is useful to top dress the surface of the soil with up to an inch or so of fresh soil. It is possible sometimes for the upper roots in a pot actually to be visible above the soil. This is an indication that top-dressing is required.

Soils

House plants, because of their limited root system, their comparatively long life and the highly artificial conditions under which they live, require a somewhat more specialised soil or rooting medium than most plants grown either for the garden or in the greenhouse. They require in general terms a soil that is rich in nourishment, open in texture and long-lasting in result. There is no question that specially prepared mixtures of high humus content are undoubtedly best for house plants, but we must recognise that it is seldom a practical proposition for the normal householder to obtain or prepare these soils without considerable difficulty. It is therefore suggested that we go to the invaluable, tailor-made, and readily obtainable John Innes composts for our soils. These composts were first devised some score or so years ago by W. J. C. Lawrence and J. Newell of the John Innes Horticultural Institution. They are completely standardised and if prepared according to recipe should be identical in all parts of the world. Unfortunately, there is no means of ascertaining whether in fact the preparation of "John Innes compost" has been correctly carried out, and some suppliers are producing a product which I fear is incorrectly labelled. There is no means of knowing this other than by the reputation of the supplier. The recipe prepared by the John Innes scientists for potting is:

7 parts by bulk of loam

3 parts peat

1 part coarse sand plus per bushel $\frac{1}{4}$ lb. John Innes
    base fertiliser

$\frac{3}{4}$ oz. chalk.

The formula for the John Innes base fertiliser is:

2 parts hoof and horn

2 parts super-phosphate of lime

1 part sulphate of potash.

It is important that these proportions should be maintained as closely as possible. Mr. Lawrence has told me "the figures given for the fertilisers are the outcome of numerous experiments, and gardeners should not try to vary the proportions on their own account. The amounts should be strictly adhered to and not merely approximated. Guesswork should not be employed either for measure of fertilisers or the soil."

Fortunately certain horticultural sundriesmen now prepare John Innes composts on a very large scale, and pack them up in amounts varying from 7 lb. to 1 cwt. It is therefore possible to buy from all good garden stores comparatively modest amounts of good standardised soil, which can be relied on in all situations and under all coditions. It is important, one might almost say vital, that in preparation the loam should be sterilised before being mixed with the other ingredients, which is one reason it is not advisable for the average gardener, however keen, to prepare his own soil mixtures. Few of us have the facilities to carry out this task accurately. A sterilised soil means that all weeds are killed, and even more important that all weed seeds are also dead. This means that our young plants or our transplants will not be smothered by weeds.

Some of the more specialist house plant nurseries, although paying tribute to the value of the John Innes mixtures, prefer in fact to use their own composts for their own plants. Indeed if the specialists there grow plants on a large scale, they will have learnt that although the John Innes recipe is on average the best for all types of plants, they can obtain better results by specialising their mixtures and providing looser, richer or heavier soils to suit the individual requirements of individual plants. This of course is to our benefit as purchasers, but we should be ill-advised to copy the specialist soil mixtures ourselves. In general it can be said that the specialist composts usually contain a higher humus content than is contained in the John Innes mixtures, and possibly some slight variation in the proportion of fertilisers in the base. No specialist house plant grower will quarrel with the suggestion that on the whole the average house plant owner can do no better than use a good John Innes compost for the entire range of his house plants.

In recent years certain no-soil mixtures have been introduced which have done away with soil, substituting in its place a sterile peat base. Fertilisers are added to give the mixture the same nutritional value as John Innes composts. Although these no-soil composts are handy in many ways, I do not think that even the makers suggest that they should be used for house plants except for their propogation, which subject I shall deal with later.

Pots and Pot Sizes

Most house plants are sold in florist shops, flower markets or nurseries as comparatively young plants in comparatively small pots. Although certain plants such as saintpaulias, cryptanthus, certain hederas, and perhaps some tradescantias may be sold in tiny pots called "thumbs," most appear in the size known technically as "60's." These are so called because 60 pots are "thrown" in unbaked clay at the same time. They are roughly 3 inches in diameter at the top of the pot. This is a fairly small size, and a "60" pot cannot be expected to maintain and nourish the roots of a strong growing plant for many months. It must also be remembered that a pot of this size can only accommodate a certain limited amount of water, and that small pots must therefore be watered more frequently than larger ones. The next size of pot generally used is the "48" or 5 inch pot, followed by the "32"— $5\frac{1}{4}$ in., "24"—$7\frac{1}{2}$ in., and so on up, if absolutely necessary, to the one with an 18 in. top diameter. This size is obviously only used under very special circumstances.

Even the manufacturers of plastic flower pots, which are being increasingly accepted and used both commercially and by the private enthusiast, retain these basic sizes as near as makes no difference. This is due to the fact that generations of growers, through practice in nurseries, have become accustomed to these sizes, and have thus become familiar with the amounts of soil and fertiliser required per pot.

Plastic pots have undoubtedly certain advantages, but they have disadvantages too. In the first place they are light, easy to handle and to clean. On the other hand, they are not porous and will accept no water through their sides. To the best of my knowledge all have drainage holes in the base. They are said to be warmer than clay pots, and cleaner in that they do not permit bacterial or fungal activity within the actual wall. You will not find on a plastic pot, for example, the green mould or moss so frequently found under greenhouse conditions on a clay pot. Consequently, certain plants such as the difficult saintpaulia, which suffers frequently from petiole rot when its leaves come into contact with the rim of the clay pot, will do better if it has a plastic pot as its more hygienic home. There is probably less wastage of plant foods in plastic pots than in clay. It is easier with plastic pots to make sure that these foods, which are always in solution, reach the root ball area.

Plant Foods

The main plant foods are nitrogen, phosphorus and potassium. Less important are calcium, magnesium, sulphur, iron, sodium, chlorine, manganese, copper, zinc and boron. The first three are present in varying amounts in all complete proprietary fertilisers, and it is important to accept the fact that, regardless of one's personal philosophy, it makes no difference whatsoever to any plant of any kind whether it receives these foods in the form of chemicals or of natural organic manure or fertilisers. The plant can use them only in solution, and the solution entering the plant's system via root hairs or leaves is exactly the same whether it comes from inorganic chemicals or organic manures or composts.

Nitrogen, the most important element in fertilisers, aids quick growth, gives a good green colour to the leaves and is essential when a plant is growing strongly. If a plant does not grow well and tends to show a yellow colour in its leaves, especially along the veins, then it is probably suffering from a nitrogen deficiency. On the other hand, if too much nitrogen is given to a plant its growth is soft and weak, the leaves are a very dark green, and flowers or fruits will be late to appear and of poor quality. The plant will be open to attack from fungoid disease and will be less resistant to cold.

Phosphorus is in some ways the natural opposite of nitrogen. It encourages maturity and ripeness in a plant, promotes flower, seed and fruit development, is essential for vigorous root growth and gives resistance to attacks of disease and to the effects of cold.

Potassium is essential for good strong growth and fine quality flowers, fruits and seeds.

In view of the fact that plants accept fertilisers only in the form of chemicals in solution, it is obvious that they can be grown without soil and with their roots merely in liquids containing these chemicals. All plants can of course be grown in this way, and generally speaking it is only the somewhat precarious balance needed between the chemicals that makes this a more difficult task than it appears on the surface.

We have grown many plants in water alone, to which have been added minute quantities of complete fertilisers, and we have successfully grown plants in a moisture retentive material such as sand, vermiculite or Florapak, again with the addition of minute quantities of a complete fertiliser. The fact that plants continue to be sold and to be grown in soil mixtures is not because soil is necessary to them, so much as the fact that it is a convenience for holding roots in position, and an invaluable aid in minimising and overcoming the mistakes we make in plant feeding and watering.

This is not the place to go into a detailed examination of soil composition and construction, but it can perhaps merely be said that a soil is a highly complex mixture varying in many ways, and containing not only minerals and organic materials, but vast quantities of active bacteria without which they would not be able to function as efficiently as they do.

Propagation

When we are growing house plants we like to know all the ways in which we can continue the life of the parent plant should it grow old and decrepit, or ways in which we may increase our stock either for our own enjoyment or to pass to friends. Fortunately, nearly all house plants can be propagated with comparative ease if the right method is adopted. Some of our plants need little or no assistance, producing offsets from their bases as a normal process of life. Others will produce their offspring from special runners, as strawberries do in the garden, and still others can be induced to bring forth young if we subject them to special treatment.

I do not propose to discuss the more difficult means of propagating house plants. Instead, a word or two about the more or less natural processes by which we can increase our stock may be helpful. With each of the individual plants mentioned in later pages, a section will deal with propagation.

We can propagate our plants (a) from offsets, (b) from leaf, stem or tip cuttings, (c) by layering (stem or air), (d) by division, and (e) by using seeds produced. For each of the plants mentioned later in this book the most effective means of propagation is indicated, and reference should be made back to this section for further details.

Offsets

Certain plants, such as *Aechmea fasciata*, produce a flower and hence seeds. Once this function has been fulfilled the plant begins to die. As the seeds are difficult to germinate, except under conditions of heat and humidity which are normally not available in our homes, the plant ensures its posterity by producing at the same time a number of children vegetatively. That is, its roots produce at the base of the parent plant one or more young plants which with the assistance of the parent's roots will grow happily to maturity. These baby plants can be allowed to remain attached to the parent, which is cut away to soil level when it begins to die. Alternatively, young plants can be removed bodily, and set into a pot of fresh soil to assume a new and individual life of their own.

In this case a sharp knife must be used to cut the young plant which is adhering to the parent. Care must, however, be taken to ensure that a strong section of root growth remains. In other words, the cut must be vertical and not horizontal, and the tender roots of the baby plant must be eased carefully from the old pot. The baby plant can be inserted into a small pot of fresh soil, watered thoroughly, and then left for the new roots to grow.

Leaf, Stem or Tip Cuttings

Though perhaps slightly more complex, the propagation of young plants by each of these methods is still not difficult. If we are to use leaf cuttings as a means of propagating *Begonia rex*, for example, there are two possible ways of proceeding. One is to take a complete leaf and spread it as flat as possible on a bed or box of damp sand or fine peat. If it does not lie flat it can be pinned to the surface by two or three pieces of wire bent hairpin-fashion. If the main veins of the leaf are slashed in several places with a sharp knife and if the sand is kept moist, then young shoots or young growths should begin at the portions of vein which have been cut. Root hairs will appear below and cling into the moist medium. When the young plants are large enough to be handled, they can be divided and potted up in the normal manner.

Alternatively, an entire leaf can be detached from a parent plant and the stem can be inserted into a container of plain water. If the junction of stem and leaf is allowed to be just under water, roots will soon be seen to be forming.

Tradescantias and several other plants will root quickly and easily if a growing tip is cut off from the parent plant and inserted into moist soil, sand, or even water alone.

A sansevieria leaf can be sliced into several pieces, each of which, when inserted for half an inch or so into moist soil, sand or peat, will produce baby plants. Pieces of stem of certain plants such as dracaenas and philodendrons will form roots if inserted once again into moist sand, soil or peat.

So many of our house plants in fact can be encouraged to reproduce themselves by means of cuttings, that it is worth-while trying to do this if one is uncertain of the correct means of propagation.

Layering

Just as certain shrubs in the garden can be layered by pressing a good shoot into the soil, so the same process can be adopted with certain house plants. It is sometimes helpful to make a slight notch or slit in the stem, at the part which will be beneath the soil. This frequently encourages quicker root growth.

A more complex method called air layering can be used in the production for example of a new India Rubber plant from one that has outgrown itself, or from which the lower leaves have dropped. In this case, the bark is removed around the main stem at a spot not less than six inches or so from the growing tip, or a notch or slit is made in the stem at the same point. This bare or slit portion of stem should be covered with a ball of moist sphagnum moss which is tied securely into position. The whole of this is then covered by tying over it a piece of polythene, so that the package is airtight, and in a matter of a few weeks new roots will form and grow into the moss. Cut this "new" plant from the parent plant immediately below the new roots. The new plant can be potted up in the normal way.

Division

Plants which reproduce themselves by means of offsets (aspidistra, sansevieria are examples) are in fact reproduced by division, so the two methods of increasing stock are almost synonymous. On the other hand some plants such as ivies and tradescantias can if desired have the roots cut or torn by hand into smaller sections each of which can be planted. This operation is exactly the same as that performed on, say Michaelmas Daisies, in the garden.

Seeds

Not very many house plants grow sufficiently ripe or mature to produce seeds. When they do or when seed is bought, it can be planted in the usual way, but it will be found as a general rule that heat is required for germination. Small electrically heated propagating cases are useful for this purpose, comparatively inexpensive, and conveniently small in size.

Pests and Diseases

Due to the reasonably uncontaminated conditions in which most house plants live, pests are of less importance than outdoors in the garden. Fortunately, nearly all commercial house plant growers find that an almost clinical cleanliness is advantageous in their glass-houses, and only very rarely are purchased house plants found to be bearing any form of pest or disease.

The comparatively dry air inside a normal home occasionally results in the appearance of a pest known as red spider. With the help of a magnifying glass it is sometimes possible to see these tiny red mites (they are not really spiders), which multiply on the surface of leaves and weave a hairy web. Leaves will turn brown and drop. Red spider will spread and develop rapidly unless checked at the earliest opportunity.

One of the best cures for red spider is a white oil emulsion called "Volck," which is helpful in fact against other house plant pests also. After being mixed with water, it is sprayed on to plants, and coats leaf and stem surfaces with a fine film of disinfectant. As it is likely to spoil furniture, it is best to do this out of doors, or to cover any surfaces which might catch droplets of the liquid with newspaper or other protection. Alternatively "Volck" can be used as a wash, a piece of cotton wool being dipped in the solution and swabbed over the leaves. Large-foliaged plants are best for this form of treatment, which also imparts a healthy gloss to the leaves.

Aphids are sometimes found on house plants, usually coming in from the garden, or from garden plants brought indoors. Once again "Volck" will clear these. The new systemic insecticides (Abol-X, Tritox) give long-term protection and are easily applied. Scale and mealy bug, both small, flat, white insects, can once again be cleared by using "Volck", although in this case treatment should be by wiping leaves, both top and lower surfaces, with a rag or sponge dipped in the solution. Scale is sometimes difficult to remove, as it clings tightly to the leaf surface, and a more vigorous wipe might be necessary, or even the dislodging of the sucker by a match stick.

Diseases of house plants are few, and the only two that need give any concern to the average house plant enthusiast are mildew and root rot. Both of these are caused by bad cultivation methods. If roots are kept too moist for long periods then root rot is almost certain to set in, and mildew may also be found. Insufficient ventilation, crowded conditions, too dry an atmosphere can each induce mildew, which is seen as a white powdery fungus on the surface of leaves. Although some improvement of this disease can be obtained by spraying with white oils, it is the conditions which have brought it about that need to be changed.

Training

Many house plants will grow to a considerable size, and

although attractive in shape when in a younger and smaller state, they sometimes lose their graceful appearance when they become old and straggly. House plants should be treated firmly and subjected to minor doses of discipline, to ensure that they grow in an attractive shape and do not exceed the bounds which must be set on them. Judicious pruning can do nothing but good. Frequently of course, the pieces cut from an over-large house plant can be rooted and used to increase one's stock. Discoloured edges to leaves can be cut cleanly away with a pair of sharp scissors before the discoloration extends further along the leaf surface.

Although training canes, wire, brackets or string sometimes look unsightly, they are nevertheless worth-while to encourage growth in the directions in which it is required, and will usually be disguised or hidden before long by new foliage.

Nomenclature

Because house plants live in the intimate atmosphere of the home, many of them have been given intimate names which may suit them because of their growing characteristics, shapes or colours, or their habits. Thus the sansevieria has been unkindly nicknamed "Mother-in-Law's Tongue" because of its shape and spiky appearance. Unfortunately, these names are not accurate, and some plants indeed may have several different nicknames. On occasions like these it is impossible for one person to know for certain which plant is meant when a nickname is used.

Latin names, difficult though they may seem to some of us, are accurate and accepted all over the world. There is an international code of horticultural nomenclature to which all plants, old and new, must adhere. In order to have formulae which are accepted all over the world, obviously certain rules must be obeyed, but so far as we

28

are concerned with house plants we can reduce these rules to one or two. We can in fact use an analogy of our own names. My family name or surname is Johns. In order to distinguish me from my wife and the other members of my family, I have been given a forename or christian name which specifies or defines me as being Leslie Johns.

In the same way, all plants are named firstly according to their genus and secondly according to their species. The sansevieria belongs to the genus of this name, after an 18th-century Prince of San Severo. There are a number of members of this genus, the best known being *Sansevieria trifasciata.*

To make things even more complex, there are several different forms or variations of *Sansevieria trifasciata.* To be technically correct, we should say that the most commonly grown form of this plant in our homes is *Sansevieria trifasciata var.* (variety) *Laurentii.* Frequently, however, the *var.* is dispensed with, so we come finally to *Sansevieria trifasciata Laurentii.* This identifies the plant with certainty all over the world, and in fact to some extent describes it.

These Latin names, though they may sometimes appear difficult in print and even more difficult to pronounce, are nothing to be afraid of. They follow logical rules and are of tremendous assistance in defining accurately what we mean. Although I shall give common names or nicknames where they exist, I shall also stick strictly to correct botanical nomenclature. Nomenclature in the field of house plants is particularly confused and open to argument because of the large numbers of new hybrids continually being produced, and for this reason I shall follow in succeeding pages the authority of the Royal Horticultural Society's Dictionary of Gardening.

2

HOUSE PLANTS IN DETAIL

Aechmea

This is a favourite plant of mine, and popular with many men because of their liking for clean-cut, regular shapes. The shiny, grey-green leaves have horizontal bands of paler colour. In rosette form, they rise from a central point to make a cup or "vase"; hence "Grecian Vase Plant." The leaves are up to two feet or so in length, and up to two inches or so wide. Slightly serrated, they are nevertheless not unpleasant to the touch and certainly will not scratch or cut the hands.

Aechmea fasciata is the most popular variety. Most aechmeas in this country are sold when the flower is beginning to develop. This grows on the end of a long stem in the centre of the "vase," and reaches upwards until it stands well above the leaves. The head of flowers is spectacular, unusual and breathtakingly beautiful. It arrives first as a spear-shaped spike or collection of spikes. Each of these sharp and spiny bracts is a delicate pink, and from each as it opens will come a tiny light purple-blue flower. These flowers will last for some weeks and will then fade. Some will fall, and the remainder can be plucked away with tweezers. This still leaves, however, the original spiny collection of pink bracts, which remains for months, quite as beautiful as many flowers.

When the bracts finally begin to die the plant itself is dying. Even in death, however, it continues to serve us, for if it has been well looked after it will throw up one, two, three or perhaps even more sideshoots. These nestle up to the original or parent plant and grow quickly. They can either be left to grow where they began their life, or they can be cut from the parent plant with a sharp knife, taking also a section of their roots. They can then be potted up in a good well-drained soil, and if given a little encouragement they will quickly make roots. Again, given good cultural conditions, one can expect to see a central flower from the young plants in the following year.

The aechmea is an easy plant to look after. It likes as much sun and light as it can get, but it will tolerate a certain amount of drought and is surprisingly hardy for a plant which comes from Mexico. Personally I like to keep the soil in the pot slightly moist, but some people say it is sufficient merely to keep the "vase" of the plant filled with water at all times. If this is kept topped up, a certain amount of moisture trickles down through the leaves to the soil below. It is perhaps as well to use tepid water during the cold days of winter for topping up the "vase."

The aechmea belongs to the family of bromeliads, and is an epiphyte, growing mainly in the branches or on the trunks of trees. Thus its roots frequently never know soil as such in the natural state, and it gets its moisture from rain and dew which it stores in the central cup or "vase." Its normal lack of soil indicates to us that it should not be over-potted, that is to say it should be kept in as small a pot as possible for as long a time as possible. In fact, as it propagates itself by offsets, these generally dictate the size of the pot rather than the root system. Managing to exist with very little water, it must obviously require very little food also. In the forests of central America the central cup of the aechmea is sometimes found to be the home of frogs or other moisture loving fauna. It is possible that the manures from these help to fertilise the plants.

Although the roots, then, serve more as an anchor for the plant than as a source of food and moisture, those plants that have been found growing on the forest floor rather than in the trees are always better in size, colour and vigour. Thus we shall benefit by paying some attention to the kind of soil we use. Usually an aechmea will grow quite satisfactorily in a normal John Innes mixture, but it will probably do better in a slightly more acid soil than in the neutral John Innes.

Aglaonema
This genus, with some 40 or so species, seems to me worthy of considerably more attention from the commercial growers than it has received so far. Of the 40 species only half a dozen can be obtained in this country, nomenclature and proper identification appear to be somewhat vague and haphazard, and the best of them, known popularly in the United States as "Chinese Evergreen," and botanically as *A. modestum*, does not appear to be listed under this name by any grower in this country.

By this complaint I do not suggest that the aglaonemas are outstandingly attractive, but they have a certain charm and are fairly tolerant on the whole of the poor conditions under which most house plants are forced to live. *A. modestum*, the "Chinese Evergreen," is said to be particularly tough, and according to the Royal Horticultural Society Dictionary, cut leaves will last for months in water.

The aglaonemas are small plants, their spear-shaped leaves growing on short stalks to a length of between five and nine inches. Under ideal conditions, such as might exist in a heated greenhouse, it is probable that some of the species might grow larger. Like most house plants they will not tolerate gas or other fumes in the atmosphere, even in the most minute quantities. If they do not like the conditions under which they are supposed to live, they will drop their leaves, and gradually a short trunk will be

Citrus nitis 'Calamondin'

Cissus discolor

Cyperus gracilis

Ficus lyrata in corner of room, F. radicans on sideboard

Cryptanthus acaulis

Begonia rex

formed with scar tissues indicating the original joints between leaf stalks and stem.

The best known variety in this country is probably *A. commutatum*, dark green with spots of paler green and silvery white. The leaves are spear-shaped, rounded at the stem end and about six inches long. It is said to have been found in the Philippine islands in 1863.

All known members of the aglaonema genus (aroids, by the way) seem to have been found in the latter half of the 19th century, heyday of the conservatory and stove house, and brought back to enjoy conditions similar in many respects to those in the forests and swamps of Malaya, Borneo and the Philippines.

Probably only under ideal conditions can an aglaonema be brought to flower and fruit in this country. The flowers are arum-like, and also monoecious, that is, each flower has only one sex, although other flowers on the same plant may have different sexes. Some authorities report that mature plants will produce clusters of scarlet berries, which links the aglaonemas with our only native English aroid, the wild arum, known popularly as "Lords and Ladies" and "Cuckoo Pint" or botanically, *Arum maculatum.*

Anthurium

Another aroid, or member of the *Araceae* or arum family, is the anthurium, popularly known as the "Piggy Tail Plant," "Flamingo Flower," or "Palette Plant." Popular names always have some visible source, and each of these is applicable because of the characteristics of the plant. "Piggy Tail Plant" refers to the short spirally twisted spadix. "Flamingo Flower" is descriptive of the brilliant pink, scarlet, white or pale green spathe which, because of its shape, also results in the name of "Palette Plant."

This, frankly, is not an easy plant to grow in the home. It likes a greater degree of warmth and humidity than we can normally give it. It is possible for us to keep an anthurium in a steady temperature of about 15-20 degrees C. or 60-70 F., but it is less easy to maintain the humidity that is necessary. The best way is to stand the pot in a tray of shingle which is always kept moist, or better still to plunge the entire pot in a larger container filled with moist peat, moss, sand or crumpled Florapak. All of these will tend to keep the roots moist, and at the same time by natural evaporation send a thin film or cloud of humidity upwards around the foliage and flowers. Thus, although the living accommodation in the house or flat will still be as warm and dry as we like it ourselves, a micro-climate of warmth and humidity will be produced around the plant itself, from which it will benefit.

In spite of all you can do to try to provide conditions which the anthurium will enjoy, it is likely to have a comparatively short life in the average home. On the other hand it will still last a great deal longer than a bunch of cut flowers, and give pleasure for the whole of this time. It is also possible to watch the plant carefully, and when it shows sign of tiredness to send it for recuperation to the greenhouse, or back to the nursery. A number of nurserymen will accept a plant for nursing, although from their point of view it is obvious that this must be done at the customer's risk and at a charge which sometimes seems to be rather high.

Practically the only anthurium that is available from nurserymen or florists as a house plant is *Anthurium scherzerianum*. This comes from Costa Rica and has a brilliantly red spathe or "flower," from which in a little curl comes the twisted spadix, orange red in colour, which actually holds the tiny and almost insignificant flowers. *A. scherzerianum* is an unusually variable plant, with up to 50 or so hybrids, and although something like 500 species of the genus Anthurium have been recognised and named, the scherzerianum is still the most popular for room cultivation, probably because it is one of the easiest to look after and because its "flower" is particularly long lasting.

It might be worth while to spend just a moment explaining the terms spathe, spadix and bract, so that we can understand the nature of this plant a little better. A spathe, then, is a part of the flower which is folded around the immature spadix. On a flower such as the arum lily, the spathe opens to reveal the spadix, but still continues to shield or shelter it around roughly half of its perimeter. With the anthurium, the spathe opens completely and lies more or less flat, with the spadix projecting above it. The spadix is a flower spike studded with tiny flowers. A bract is a modified leaf found just underneath a flower or cluster of flowers. It is sometimes highly coloured, and, as in the case of the poinsettia (*Euphorbia pulcherrima*), is frequently taken for the flower itself.

Aphelandra

It is now five or six years since the aphelandra first appeared in quantity as a house plant in this country. It made a tremendous impact at first, and was to be seen everywhere, for the vividly striped leaves and the bright cockscomb of yellow flower were so dramatic and so unusual that they won immediate acceptance regardless of unfamiliarity. This unfamiliarity was the undoing of the plant, which proved somewhat temperamental, and after the first flush of popularity waned the aphelandra went through a period of disgrace. As might have been expected, the attractions of the plant overcame its drawback, and as indoor gardeners came to understand it better it came gradually back into favour.

The aphelandra belongs to a genus of about 60 species, all originating in the tropical areas of central America.

Although some of these species are occasionally to be seen in greenhouses, *A. squarrosa Louisae* is the only one generally to be seen in the flower shops and in the home. It is named after a recent Queen of the Belgians, and there is a similar variety, *A. s. Leopoldii*, named after the first Belgian king of that name. Louisae, however, is undoubtedly the better grower, the easier to manage and the more attractive of the two. In 1963 I obtained a new aphelandra called *A. uniflora* (though I can find no reference to this name in my books), which appears in some ways to have better habits than Louisae, and which may yet supplant it in favour. I had this plant in my London home for several months during the winter of 1963, and it flowered well, kept its foliage and was generally of an equable nature.

The aphelandra flowers in the autumn, taking up to a month to do so. The flowers appear in the centres of yellow bracts which grow to a sort of four-sided pyramid, and even after the flowers have faded, the bracts will continue to be showy and attractive. They should not be allowed to grow on the plant for too long, however, but as they gradually turn green they should be removed to allow new side shoots to grow.

The main thing to understand about the aphelandra is that it is delicate and must be treated carefully. It must not suffer draughts. It must never be allowed to become dry at the roots. On the other hand it must never get too wet. It will tolerate quite low temperatures, but will sulk or die if temperatures are allowed to fluctuate widely between mid-day warmth and midnight cold. It should be given plenty of light and be placed near a window, but not so near that it suffers either from burning sunlight or from frost.

Fortunately, the aphelandra foliage is attractive in itself, without the benefit of its even more unusual and attractive flower. The flower itself is long lasting, but the foliage is what makes the plant. Even without the flower the aphelandra would still be successful, and with a certain amount of care it can be retained in the home in good condition for a year or more. Remember, however, that aphelandras fall into the category of the "temporary" plants; that is, those that will survive and give pleasure in the home under normal conditions for many months, but which cannot be expected to live for year after year as some house plants do. Be prepared to pay the £1 or so that an aphelandra costs and is worth, and realise that this is mere rent for up to a year of sterling service. When the plant has given this service, then re-invest.

Certainly do not attempt to propagate from your own plants unless you have a heated greenhouse or a propagating case, for you will be disappointed. Prolong the life of your existing plant by feeding it with weak liquid manure while it is in flower, by keeping it out of draughts, by never allowing it to dry out, and by pinching out the flowering bract when it has passed its best.

Araucaria

To include a tree which will grow to 200 feet in height in this list of house plants may seem ridiculous, but I hasten to say that under the artificial conditions imposed by being confined to a pot and living-room atmospheres, more reasonable sizes may be expected. I must admit, however, that I should not have considered the araucaria suitable, except that it had been highly recommended to us by no less an expert than Tom Rochford, largest grower of house plants in the world. We were at his nurseries, and when we were leaving, with characteristic generosity he filled our car with plants. "And take this to Jeremy," he said, referring to our young son, who was then about three years old, "He won't be able to kill it."

The plant for Jeremy was an *Araucaria excelsa*, a Norfolk Island Pine, similar in many ways to the familiar Monkey Puzzle Tree which we see in so many front gardens in this country. It is not easily available and may involve a search, but as it is quite distinctive and grows easily in the home it is worth the trouble.

The tree is, of course, a conifer. It has beautifully balanced and symmetrical branches reaching out on each side of the main stem. These branches are a glaucous green in colour, and fresher and brighter at the growing tips. Araucaria likes to be kept moist at the roots, but otherwise makes few demands.

The soil used should be slightly acid, and open in texture. Several varieties with slight differences of colour are available.

Aspidistra

Once the subject of music hall jokes, the aspidistra to-day is a much more serious subject. This is because the demand for it as a house plant far exceeds the supply. I mentioned this fact some years ago in a well-known national periodical, and was immediately inundated with letters from readers. There were two types of letter, roughly equal in number. One said, "I have an old aspidistra I shall be glad to divide for you," and the other said, "If you hear of an aspidistra about, will you let me have one?" I did my best to match "giving" readers with "seeking" readers.

The reason for the shortage of aspidistra plants is simply that it is a slow grower. Nurserymen just cannot grow plants quickly enough for them to be economic. With the cost of greenhouses at a minimum figure of £20,000 an acre, no grower can afford to lock up this valuable space with a crop which will take years, instead of months, to bring to saleable maturity.

The aspidistra is a member of the lily family, a genus of only about four species. The house plant is *A. lurida*, which has long, spear-like green leaves on a short stalk. *A. lurida variegata*, the variegated form with alternate green and white vertical stripes, is even more scarce and we have, in fact, been offered considerable sums of money for our own single plant.

"Cast Iron Plant" and "Parlour Palm" were two of the names given to the aspidistra when it was at the height of its popularity during the Victorian era. The plant was to be seen everywhere. As it can by no means be described as a striking or a beautiful plant, there must have been a reason for its popularity. The explanation was, of course, that it would withstand gas fumes. Many Victorian homes were lit by gas, and as even one part in a million of gas in the atmosphere is sufficient to affect many house plants, the aspidistra was unusual in its ability to live happily in rooms with very great concentrations of gas in the air. It would also withstand long periods of neglect, growing away in soil either bone dry or flooded. The plant is very hardy, and one or two of ours have, in fact, survived a complete winter out of doors in London.

Because it will survive neglect is no reason why the aspidistra should not be treated as kindly as are other more delicate house plants. It will, in fact, grow better and more quickly, look better and live longer if treated gently. It likes a good rich soil and plenty of water at all times. It will benefit from a spell in the garden or on the balcony during the summer, particularly during periods of soft rain. If looked after well the aspidistra will produce its own flowers which are small, inconspicuous, and placed low down near the soil.

Propagation of the aspidistra is by division and the taking of suckers. An old plant in a large pot (as so many of them are) can be split up into a surprising number of new plants, and a new plant will live happily in a small pot for many years without re-potting.

Begonia

Named after a 17th-century Governor of French Canada, Michel Begon, the begonia belongs to a genus of some 350 species, several of which make interesting and attractive house plants. The flowering begonias useful in this way are dealt with separately, and I propose to discuss in this section only the foliage or *Begonia rex* varieties.

Once again here we run into difficulties of nomenclature, for although most of the decorative foliage begonias have been lumped together in the public minds as *Begonia rex*, this is not strictly correct. *Begonia rex* is a typical species, it is true, but there are certainly very many others, and also very many hybrids, some of which, to add to our many troubles, have been incorrectly named.

Almost all the begonias which are useful to us as house plants, because of their beautiful or interesting leaf shapes and colours fall into the rhizomatous group, as opposed to the tuberous, fibrous or bulbous rooted types. They have all come from the tropics, American, Eastern and Asian. They are characterised by lop-sided leaves, roughly triangular in shape, which are frequently toothed and are always coloured with irregular bands or splotches of green, silver, purple, scarlet, or red. Textures may vary from the rough and hairy to the smooth and indeed almost metallic.

Although many of these have come to be called *Begonia rex* regardless of their species, the following can sometimes be found correctly named: *cathayana* (green and crimson); *coccinea* (red); *daedalea* (green, brown, scarlet, hairy); *decora* (red with yellow veins); *feastii* (mainly red, hairy); *haageana* (red and purple); *heracleifolia* (bronze-green, hairy); *imperalis* (two-toned green); *metalica* (green with metallic sheen); *masoniana* ("Iron Cross").

I fear that our own findings do not bear out the common advice given by most experts about *Begonia rex* and similar foliage varieties. We are told that the plants are somewhat delicate, that they require some degree of humidity, that they will not succeed in direct sunlight, that they need constant temperatures, and that they will not tolerate any gas or industrial dirt in the atmosphere. But although we grow *Begonia rex* both in London and in the country under totally different conditions and circumstances, we have always found them to be exceedingly easy and tolerant plants for the home. In the country the plants may have dirt, gas and fume free conditions, but on the other hand our plants are in south facing windows where they get the full sun; they get periods of two or more weeks when they receive no water at all. They are warm while we are in residence, and can get very cold while we are away. In London the plants again face south, though with a lesser degree of direct sunlight; they have a less humid atmosphere; they get the air pollution inevitable right in the centre of London. Yet all of our begonias are simple to grow, making no demands of time or care, all of which has induced in us the opinion that these simply lovely plants are among the easiest to look after and most rewarding of all.

Our begonias generally get a certain amount of feeding during the summer, but are not in as good a soil as they should be. They like a really rich loam with enough sharp sand to make the mixture open and freely drained. They are said to like an overhead spray of clean water every now and again, but none of ours have ever received this.

The "correct" way of propagating foliage begonias is to slash the main veins of a leaf in several places and then lay the leaf flat on a bed of moist sand or peat. At the slashed points new plants will grow. We have had little or no success with this method, although it is only fair to say that we have not tried it under the ideal conditions of a heated propagating case or even a greenhouse. What we have found is that a single leaf removed from a plant and stood with its stem in plain water will soon root, and can then be potted up in the normal manner.

Although most varieties of foliage begonias will produce flowers, these are of a minor and insignificant nature. Usually a dirty white or grey in colour, they have no beauty and may be ignored. On the other hand, when the plants do come into flower it is important to realise that they are going through a period of considerable strain and exhaustion, and should be treated gently and given plenty of moisture and rather more lavish feeding than is normally the case.

Beloperone

Although this plant is grown mainly for its flowers, I have listed it under foliage rather than flowering plants because the flowers themselves are insignificant, the bracts surrounding them being far more important. These bracts, a brownish pink in colour, droop downwards from the plant in a series of overlapping scales which bear a remarkable similarity to a prawn or shrimp. Hence the popular name "Shrimp Plant." These groups of bracts are normally some three inches long, although they will grow larger if the plant is greenhouse grown.

The beloperone is a shrubby plant with soft green leaves. It grows well and easily and likes plenty of light. A place in a good sunny window is right for it, and there the bracts will gain in colour, losing their brownish tinge and taking on a much more attractive pinkish hue. It also likes a certain amount of air, but not draughts, so when it is in the window only the upper part should be opened, and then only in the warmer months. Although the plant will tolerate quite cool conditions, it does not like changes of atmosphere, and the bracts will sometimes drop off in these circumstances.

Grown well the beloperone will reach some three feet in height, and as the bracts droop downwards and the stem is rather soft and weak, the plant frequently looks at its best placed fairly high. We once kept a plant in the bowl of an antique standard oil-lamp, where it looked most attractive.

Mexico is its home, and it was found and brought to this country as lately as 1936. It has not, I believe, had the recognition it deserves, for it is both pleasant to look at and easy to care for. It has the reputation of being so floriferous as to make it difficult to take cuttings.

The soil should be rich and open in texture, and the plant likes plenty of water. As it grows and flowers so freely it needs keeping under control, and it is best to do this by pinching out new shoots in spring and clipping back in autumn. New plants can easily be raised from cuttings in the spring. Feed fairly well during the summer months when most growth is appearing.

Billbergia

Named in honour of the Swedish botanist J. G. Billberg, the billbergia has been with us almost 100 years. It is one of the comparatively few terrestrial bromeliads and is quite easy to grow in the average home. It is surprisingly tolerant of cool and dry conditions, and quickly and easily throws suckers which can be detached for further propagation.

The plant is composed of a rosette of narrow leaves which spring up from a central "vase" to a length of a foot or so. These leaves are a pale grey-green and end in a sharp point. The flowers, as usual, spring from the centre of the "vase" and grow on long stalks to about the height of the leaves before appearing in colour. The tubular flowers, together with the bracts, sepals and petioles, appear to be at once blue, yellow, green and red. These flowers last quite well, certainly for a fortnight or more, and in this case when they begin to die the main plant does not die but lives on. As in the case of nearly all bromeliads, the plant will throw a number of offsets as its flowers begin to die. These should be allowed to stay on the mother plant until they reach a fair size, rather than be removed at once. When they are fairly well grown they can be gently twisted off the parent plant, trimmed of their lower leaves, and planted in a separate pot of well-drained soil, preferably, though not necessarily, with some bottom heat.

Because of the long, delicate stem on which the flowers grow, the most popular of the billbergias has been called *B. nutans*, or "nodding." This plant is generally the only one available, though it is sometimes possible to get a hybrid called *B. windii*, which is similar in many respects but has slightly larger flowers and a more dwarf or spreading habit.

Unlike many of the epiphytic bromeliads, the billbergias have narrow leaves which do not make a satisfactory "vase" that can be filled with water. The amount it will take in the vase is comparatively insignificant and the soil must also be moistened. Overhead spraying is appreciated but is not vital, and as the plants like to be moist a liberal mixture of peat in the potting soil will be helpful.

Caladium

I must confess to a feeling of slight guilt at including the caladium in this list of house plants, for as it dies down each winter and as it is frankly a really difficult plant to

44

grow from year to year I question whether it really falls
into the category of a plant for the average home. The
reason why it is included, however, will be made evident
by a glance at the photograph of the foliage. Surely it is
one of the most beautiful of all the foliage plants.

The caladium is an aroid, coming mainly from Brazil
and British Guiana, and requiring the sort of temperature
and humidity from us that it originally found there. With
a specially heated greenhouse it is possible to grow the
plant from its dormant tuber each year, but as few of us
these days have greenhouses it is better if we buy the
caladium anew each year. Plants begin to be available in
late spring or early summer, and will last the whole of the
summer before beginning to fade. Even in the summer, a
constant draught-free temperature and a relatively high
degree of humidity are necessary to keep the plant in good
condition.

The splendid leaves of the caladium spring from a
short stem. They are nearly always shaped like a broad
arrow-head, heavily veined and coloured from cream to
red. To keep the gorgeous colour of the leaves the plant
should be given as much light as possible, though not
direct and burning sunlight. The plant requires plenty of
water in its early days when it is still growing, but its in-
take should be slowed down when it reaches maturity, and
then gradually reduced as the days get shorter.

Many old-time gardeners have been so excited by
caladiums that they have bred many new hybrid plants.
Some of these are incorrectly named, and the whole
question of nomenclature here is rather hazy. But the
plants are wonderful indeed and it will be tragic if the
passing of the stove house and the conservatory means
that the caladium also disappears.

Calathea

This genus of a hundred or so species of gorgeously coloured foliage plants comes from the maranta family (q.v.). There is, in fact, only a technical, botanical difference between the two, and many calatheas are listed in catalogues as marantas, though the reverse is less often the case.

The calathea is attractive mainly because of its brilliantly and unusually marked leaves, which are blotched, zoned, lined, striped and margined with colours from green through to purple. Sometimes the leaf colouring varies according to the maturity of the plant and will change almost from week to week. Sometimes leaves are one basic colour on top and another beneath. But whatever the coloration, the contrasts are almost always vivid and spectacular.

The calatheas are not difficult to grow indoors, so long as attention is paid to protection from direct sunlight and from draughts. They like plenty of moisture and their roots should never be permitted to dry out. These roots are of a thick, fleshy nature, somewhat brittle to the touch, and as the plants regularly outgrow their pots so that they need moving on annually, it is necessary to re-pot very carefully. An open-textured soil in which the roots can move freely is necessary, and in view of their liking for moisture it is also necessary to use a greater proportion of peat than for most plants. This peat should preferably be of a granular rather than powdery nature, so that it will not compact and so obstruct the roots in their growth.

In general, re-potting is necessary not so much because the roots are pot-bound, but because the foliage has grown so thick and spreading that more room is required at the top of the pot rather than inside it. At the time of re-potting it is advisable to decide whether to divide the

46

plant and so make more, or whether to maintain the same plant in a larger pot and allow the leaves to grow even larger.

Comparatively few calathea species are to be found to-day except in the nurseries of specialists, and most of the more popular varieties stem from *C. ornata*, green, white and purple. *C. makoyana*, known in America as the "Peacock" plant, has earned its name by virtue of the tints and shades of greens, pinks and purples which colour the top and under surfaces of its leaves. Difficult to obtain at the moment, some nurserymen are busy propagating makoyana vegetatively, and it should be more generally available very shortly. More easily bought is *C. zebrina*, soft and velvety in appearance, with lime-green background and regular blotches of textured brown.

Chlorophytum

Nearly all house plants should be so placed in the home that they can be looked at from eye level or looked down on. The colouring, shape and texture of the foliage can best be enjoyed from these angles, and when the plant is below eye level then one is able to look right into the bright centre of "vase" of such a plant as the nidularium.

The chlorophytum is an exception to this rule, for it is best displayed just above the head, where a mature plant will hang down over the pot or container, and its long arching stems with the baby plantlets at the end will flow gracefully above and around the grass-like foliage. The best known species is the popular *C. comosum variegatum*, which has light green spiky, grass-like leaves with alternate lines of cream or white. The white stems of a mature plant grow upwards, and then as they become heavy with the tiny plantlets at their ends they begin to arch over and hang below the level of the pot. By chance one day we placed one of our several plants in the empty top of an antique oil lamp holder some six feet high, in our home in the country. This proved to be the perfect position for it.

Although the chlorophytum has achieved great popularity throughout the country, it is too seldom realised that the attractive stems with their tufts of tiny leaves at the ends present us with an almost foolproof method of propagating the plant. At the end of these stems, the little tuft of leaves is in fact a baby plant complete with roots, which are easily visible as the plant grows older. If this baby plantlet is allowed to rest in a pot of fairly dry and porous soil it will quickly reach out its roots and anchor itself. The stem can then be cut and a new plant will soon be in being. The baby plantlets actually follow the production of flowers, but as the latter are small and white and difficult to distinguish against the light-coloured grassy foliage they are sometimes overlooked completely.

The chlorophytum is easy to grow, tolerant of sun or shade, careless of changes of temperature, preferring plenty of water during summer months but accepting quite happily occasional periods of drought. It likes a fairly rich and open soil, though we have proved that it will grow in pure peat. It is a plant which tries always to give of its best and which responds magnificently to the provision of the conditions most suited to it. Give it a rich sandy loam, keep the roots moist, and it will grow from an undistinguished tuft of pale grass to a sunburst of flowing green and white foliage.

Cissus

Originally classified as a vine or vitis, the cissus has a climbing habit which is acknowledged in its name, which comes from the Greek *Kissos*, meaning ivy. The genus contains about 200 species. We are concerned here with one in

Azaleas

Tillandsia lindeniana

Platycerium

Little bowl of peperomia, hedera and bromeliad; narciss growing in pebbles and water; Cyclamen decora

particular, and with two or three others which are regarded as difficult but are sometimes highly attractive.

Cissus antarctica is one of the better known and more popular of the house plants mainly available to us at remarkably reasonable prices in the markets and flower shops of this country. Known popularly as the "Kangaroo Vine," it obviously comes from the southern hemisphere. It is a climber, scrambling upwards and supporting itself by means of vine-like tendrils. Its leaves are oval in shape, toothed or notched, and from one to four inches in length, depending on the skill with which it is grown. It is an easy plant, tolerant of all the normal stresses of living-room conditions.

I must confess, to my shame and disappointment, that in spite of its easy cultivation I cannot for some reason successfully grow *Cissus antarctica*. I cannot understand this, having tried for ten years or more, and having experimented with many different types of treatment. I have tried to grow it in town and in country, in light and in shade, in moist or dry conditions, in the heat and in the cold, but some insensitivity in my soul prevents me from making a success with it. I can keep a cissus for months or even years, but it will not grow as lushly or vigorously as I know it should. After only a few weeks it will begin to shed its leaves and look naked and unhappy. I make this confession more as a curious observation on my own deficiencies than as any suggestion that antarctica itself is in any way a difficult plant to grow, and I hope that readers will not be deterred from making use of this particularly attractive plant.

When purchased, the cissus is likely to be in a 60 pot and about 18 inches tall. It will be supported by a central green cane, to which it is held by two or more wire clips. It will grow in this pot quite happily for at least six months. It can either be allowed to climb farther up the stake with which it is provided or the clips can be removed, when it will trail or sprawl in a graceful and attractive manner.

If a really large plant is desired it can be re-potted yearly into one size larger pot each time. It can be induced, with little or no trouble, to grow six or more feet tall. Although it can be very attractive trained up a central pillar or support, it often looks even better with the individual trails climbing up separate supports, so that it eventually covers a complete wall.

In the summer months the cissus will require plenty of water and a fortnightly feed. It should not be allowed to dry out completely, but on the other hand it definitely does not like to be drowned. In the winter it is advisable to let the pot dry out almost completely before rewatering. It will cheerfully withstand cold weather but it does not like draughts. Normally the leaves are a dark green, but the young foliage as it appears has a much more delicate tint of this colour, and the tendrils are tan or cinnamon, with an almost hairy surface.

Another member of the cissus genus is *C. discolor*. This is admittedly an exceedingly difficult plant to grow for long periods under normal home conditions. I can remember, however, my first experience of it and my own delight in the sheer magnificence of its foliage. The leaves are in the shape of a narrow heart. Their underside is a uniform ruby red. The leaf surface is crinkled, with a dominant mid-rib from which, in herring-bone fashion, project slightly raised and crinkled divisions. In its various sections the upper leaf is silver, green, ruby, purple, pink and white. It has probably the most beautiful leaf colouring of any of our house plants. As with so many beautiful things it is not long lasting. Even with meticulous care discolor tends to lose many of its leaves during winter, a deciduous habit which some of our commercial growers would give a fortune to be able to breed out. It is again a climber, but trails attractively and is said to be wonderful in hanging baskets.

Another member of the same genus is *C. sicyoides*. It is easier to grow than discolor, though not as straightforward as antarctica. Its leaves are a simple dark green, but differ from antarctica in being divided into five sections. This makes it slightly less leaf-covered than antarctica and hence less useful, perhaps, as a house plant.

C. striata, final member of the genus, is almost a miniature of sicyoides, for the leaves are of the same shape, colour and appearance. They are, however, rather less than half as large, but fortunately considerably more profuse or lavish in their production, so that the plant is well covered.

Citrus

In Victorian days and even earlier, orange trees were a popular subject for growing in the conservatory or the "orangery." However, the lack of space in our present-day homes has done away with these invaluable aids to plant growing, and the extent of our skill in this line is usually limited to the germination of a pip. In recent months, however, a miniature orange tree has been presented to the British public as a house plant, and because of its attractive appearance and its ability to take to normal living-room conditions it is meeting with considerable success. It is known as *Citrus nitis* "*Calamondin.*" Unfortunately I can find no authority for this name in any of my reference books, and must presume it is a recently developed hybrid.

There is no question, however, but that this citrus is very much a member of the orange, lemon and lime family. Sold in a small pot, it is normally one to two feet in height, branched, and bearing a number of small orange fruits about one inch in diameter. These are not, by the way, particularly edible, being very sour and bitter to the taste. The plant has also the engaging habit of bearing both fruit and flower at the same time. The flowers sometimes need to be sought out, for they are inconspicuous, small and white, but they are very sweetly scented, as one might expect of orange blossom.

Under the artificial conditions of the living-room the flowers sometimes fail to be pollinated, in which case a little aid is required. A camel hair paint brush or the traditional rabbit's paw can simply be used to transfer pollen from the stamen of one flower to the pistil of another. A successfully pollinated flower will begin to swell into a potential fruit in a matter of only a few days.

This citrus likes plenty of light. To accept normal room temperatures the root ball must never be allowed to dry out, neither must the plant be allowed to become frosted. During the warm summer months it can go outdoors, before the colder days develop. It will probably be found that on first buying this citrus it drops its leaves and looks very uncomfortable. This is due to a natural resentment of changes of temperature and humidity. Normally the plant adjusts itself in a week or two and begins to look healthier.

The plant will normally exist in its original pot for up to two years after purchase. As might be expected it will require some gentle feeding, particularly during the summer months. If the plant is still growing and healthy after two years it should be re-potted, using a slightly more acid soil mixture than the neutral John Innes. Extra peat can be added, or a tiny dose of the new sequestrine or aluminium sulphate might prove useful. The need for a slightly more acid medium can be seen immediately from a yellowing of the foliage.

The citrus enjoys a humid atmosphere, and it may sometimes be found helpful to give it a slight spray of clean tepid water from an atomiser. If the leaves have dropped and shoots appear to be bare, the little tree can be pruned to shape during the winter months, when it is comparatively dormant.

Coleus

Coleus blumei is one of about 150 species of a genus which belongs to the *Labiatae*. It came originally from Java, and is known by the brilliant colours of its foliage, yellow, green, pink, red and purple. All these colours and their intermediates are represented. At one time the coleus was tremendously popular and far more varieties were seen than can be bought to-day. The reason for the gradual disappearance of these plants is that they are not really suitable for the garden unless they are grown by experts, such as are employed by the various parks departments.

Those who like the "Ornamental Nettle" or coleus, like it for its vivid leaf colourings, not for the flowers, which are comparatively unimportant and should be pinched out when they appear, in order to give the more important parts of the plant a better chance of showing off. Unfortunately, even with flowers removed and under the best conditions, the coleus is apt to become leggy and ungainly, growing upwards and losing its original beauty. Frequent attention, such as pinching out tips to keep the plant bushy and the leaves large and bright, will help considerably.

The coleus is easy to root, even in plain water, and this enables us to keep a large stock of new plants coming on to replace those that lose their first freshness.

Croton or Codiaeum

As if things were not difficult enough for us in the nomenclature of house plants, the showy-leafed plant we know as a croton is not, in fact, a croton at all but a codiaeum.

Why it should have been given the name of a different genus entirely, and why that name should have stuck, is more than I (and many other authorities) can say.

Fortunately there is only one species of codiaeum in general cultivation and only one variety, so we have to cope only with the name *Codiaeum variegatum pictum*. But there are a tremendous number of forms of this plant, some of which quite incorrectly have been given their own names as though they were species. The wide range of forms means that we can have codiaeums with leaves of green, yellow, gold, orange, scarlet, pink or purple, and many other intermediates, all of them being spotted or streaked with these colours. Even the shapes of the leaves differ.

Codiaeums are not easy to keep for long periods indoors. New forms are appearing which are more tolerant of home conditions, but most tend to lose their lower leaves after a few weeks. The main reason for this is that they hate changes of temperature. On the whole they like it warm and fairly humid, but they will tolerate cooler conditions than was once thought. Unfortunately temperatures are apt to vary at different times of the day in most homes and this is the main reason why codiaeums are difficult to raise.

Pot-grown plants are usually seen with a single stem, making them somewhat tree-like. By pinching out the growing top it is quite possible to make the plant more bushy in habit. They grow quickly and root easily, so if the lower leaves drop due to normal temperature changes, it is not difficult to cut off the leafy top, pot it up and grow it into a larger plant. There is one drawback here, however, which is easily enough overcome once you know the answer. The codiaeum belongs to the family *euphorbiaceae*, the spurge family, most of which "bleed" when cut. It is vital to stop this exudation of sap, and the best way to do it quickly is to dip the cut and bleeding end into powdered charcoal or fine sand.

As they possess such brilliantly coloured leaves, it is only to be expected that the codiaeums require as much light as possible. Direct sunlight is not advised, but otherwise the plants should be placed right in a window. They should also be given a light spray with clean tepid water at frequent intervals. Feed them when they are in strong growth.

Cryptanthus

The name of this plant comes from the Greek *krypto*, to hide, and *anthos*, flower. The reason for the name is that the small green or white flowers are normally hidden in the bracts at the centre. In the shape of a flattish rosette, the plant has been compared in appearance to a star-fish.

The genus is a small one containing only a dozen or so plants, of which perhaps half can be more or less readily obtained from house plant specialists. They are terrestrial bromeliads, quite small in size and with an equally small root system. They live mainly in rock crevices and are accustomed to living happily with very little moisture. One of our own plants has been growing for many months merely tied to a branch of driftwood. It probably gets no more than a light sprinkling of water once a month, yet it still appears to be quite healthy.

One of its common names is "Earth Star" and it lies snugly on the surface of the soil with its flat foliage. It's colours are usually dull, green, white, rose, red or brown in various bands and stripes. It should be noted perhaps, that although the cryptanthus will live quite happily in sunlight or in shade, the brightness of its colours increases with the amount of light it gets.

Although I have not heard of other plants growing in

the same way, our cryptanthus on the tree branch has grown not only outwards but upwards. The central portion of the rosette has extended itself to form almost a miniature stem. The plant is now, in fact, not in the familiar star-fish shape but is forming a flattened cone.

Perhaps the most popular cryptanthus is *bivittatus*. The leaves of this are usually four to six inches long, making a flattened rosette nine to twelve inches in diameter. The most popular variety is *rosea-pictus*, dull brown and pink in colour. *C. zonatus* is about the same size, with the leaves possibly a little wider. Green and grey are the two main colours, though other varieties may include brown and red.

Although not spectacular by any means, the cryptanthus has a certain quaint and diminutive charm of its own, and its sturdy ability to fend for itself commends it for special positions in the home where watering is particularly difficult. It is also useful as a soil coverer at the base of a tall naked stemmed plant.

It is propagated by means of offsets, which, when they have reached a certain maturity, can be cut away and inserted singly in pots holding a fairly rich but very well-drained compost. Although the cryptanthus will live in quite low temperatures, it prefers some heat after transplanting.

Ctenanthe

The ctenanthe is a member of the maranta family, to which also belongs the calathea. In fact the ctenanthe is so similar in some respects to the calathea, and its own name is so difficult to pronounce, that it frequently travels under that name.

They are difficult plants to grow indoors for long periods, because they like warmth and humidity, but their leaf colourings are so delicate and attractive that it is worth the effort. The best way to keep them is to plunge the pots in moist peat or similar material, so that the roots never dry out, and so that a certain moist micro-climate may envelop the foliage. A spray with clean tepid water is also helpful during the summer months. Contrary to more normal practice for coloured foliage plants, it is not wise to give the ctenanthe too much light. If direct sunlight hits the leaves they are apt to curl, close and die.

The varieties most frequently seen are *C. lubbersiana*, which has long, narrow, pale green leaves with darker green markings; *C. oppenheimiana*, green and silver-green with purple underleaf; *C. oppenheimiana tricolor*, pale green with irregular splashes of white and pink, a most beautiful plant.

Cyperus

The cyperus belongs to the family *Cyperaceae*, a family of monocotyledons containing about 2,500 species. Cyperus itself is a genus of some 400 species. We are, however, concerned here with only one species, *C. diffusus*.

The cyperus is a rush or grass. The water or bog plant diffusus is a miniature growing like a tiny umbrella frame. Another member of the genus is *C. papyrus*, the Egyptian paper reed, which, growing on a river bank, was probably the hiding place of the baby Moses of the Bible.

C. diffusus will grow in almost any soil, but must obviously be kept constantly moist. It dislikes the sun. It has a single stem with some grass-like leaves growing to a height of four to eight inches. From each branch at the top a number of narrow leaves spread out like the spokes of an umbrella. The flowers are small and inconspicuous, but once again the plant has certain charm and is valuable largely because it cannot be over-watered. There is a variety, *C. variegatus*, which has white stripes on the foliage.

Dieffenbachia

Not one of the easiest of our house plants, the dieffenbachia is, however, one of the most attractive and one
which is gaining increasing attention. It is named after a
gardener called Dieffenbach, who nearly 150 years ago was
in charge of the plants at the Palace of Schönbrunn,
Vienna. It has the common name "Dumb Cane," because
of the poisonous nature of its sap, which causes intense
pain and swelling of the tongue if it is taken internally. It is
an aroid and one of a genus of about 20 species. The
leaves of this fleshy plant are in the shape of a broad spear,
spotted, striped or speckled with white or yellow, and up to
a foot or so long.

As a general rule most dieffenbachias are rather difficult
in their young state, as they like plenty of humidity in
the air and a complete absence of draughts or atmospheric
pollution. When they are more or less mature they are
considerably more tolerant, although they still dislike
draughts, low temperatures and any dryness at their
roots. It is therefore advisable to purchase only older (and
more expensive) plants.

The dieffenbachias are rather difficult to name with any
certainty, for there seems to be a certain ignorance among
nurserymen about the different species. This is perfectly
understandable in view of the fact that some of the species
are polymorphous and still in a state of evolutionary
change. The best known dieffenbachia, however, is *picta*,
which has a dozen or more varieties. Normally the leaves
are dark green, spotted with cream and white mainly
about the prominent mid-rib. The leaves are large and in
the shape of an oblong lance or spear. *D. bowmanii* is
even larger, with leaves a foot or so long and three or four
inches wide. It has irregular light and dark green markings.

The dieffenbachias will sometimes grow quite tall, the

new leaves growing from the centre of the plant in a long tightly coiled spiral of a tender pale green, and gradually opening to the normal shape and size.

The plant can be propagated by suckers from the base, by top cuttings or merely by planting a piece of the stem with a good bud on it. In each case a temperature of up to 80 degrees is required, as well as very humid conditions.

Dizygotheca

Dizygotheca elegantissima, the only variety of this genus which can be grown as a house plant, is usually seen in the form of a little tree on a single stem. The beauty of the plant is in the foliage, which is a dark copper colour and which is lacy, fern-like, toothed and very delicate.

Not an easy plant to grow in the home, the dizygotheca likes a certain amount of warmth, and humid conditions. A daily spray with clean tepid water during the summer months will help the plant to retain its foliage, and the pot should be plunged in moist peat or stood on a moist gravel bed so that a certain amount of humid air can encircle the foliage.

Dracaena

Belonging to the lily family, the dracaenas once again suffer from difficulties of nomenclature. Fortunately this need not trouble us, unless we intend to go more thoroughly into details of the cultivation of dracaenas than we can do here. As a rule the plants are not easy to grow in the home. Some of the latest hybrids have, however, made distinct advances in toughness, and nurserymen are showing a greater interest in the genus as its possibilities become more clearly seen.

The dracaenas are grown mainly for their ornamental and sometimes highly coloured foliage. They used to be cultivated in the old stove houses, but with improved techniques of growing, nearly all will live and thrive in a normal greenhouse to-day. Some forms are garden plants, and *D. draco*, the "Dragon Tree" from which comes "dragon's blood," is said to be hardy in Cornwall and the Scilly Isles. The garden forms are, of course, much larger plants than those we grow indoors, though even some of these will grow to four feet or so under equable conditions. The Victorians were fond of bringing some of these larger plants from their stove houses into their dining-rooms for particularly festive occasions, when their decorative foliage created the right atmosphere of opulence.

The dracaenas we most frequently see, and can most easily obtain from our markets and florist shops, include: *D. godseffiana*, more squat than most dracaenas, and with oval leaves of dark green spotted with cream or gold; *D. sanderiana*, with long narrow leaves edged with white; *D. deremensis*, very like a palm in shape, with grey-green long leaves with a dark green margin; and *D. goldieana*, with shorter, wider leaves, green, gold and silver in exotic stripes.

All the dracaenas like some warmth and plenty of light, but we have successfully grown several for long periods without giving them undue coddling. Although they like humidity, there is a danger that if they are sprayed water will lodge in the leaf axils and so cause rotting. This is less of a problem in summer than in winter, but still something to be watched.

Propagation of dracaenas is a simple matter if the correct apparatus is available, for they like plenty of warmth, some humidity and some heat under their new roots. Stems of old plants should be cut into short portions some two or three inches long, and planted in moist peat or light soil. They readily form roots under the right conditions. Although I have not yet tried it, I am confident that cuttings of this sort placed with moist peat in a plastic bag, and hung in a warm spot, will succeed in sending out their roots and forming new plants. Tip rootings can also be taken in the usual way.

Fatshedera

Although the fatshedera has become very popular because of its appearance and its tolerant nature, it is in fact a somewhat rare specimen. It is a hybrid, a cross between a fatsia and a hedera or ivy. Known technically as a bi-generic hybrid, it was formed by the crossing of two plants in entirely separate genera, *Fatsia japonica var. moseri* and the Irish Ivy or *Hedera hibernica*. Hybrids of this nature are really quite rare except in the extremely complex and experimental field of orchids.

Not particularly spectacular, the fatshedera is quite easy to grow, as it has taken on some of the best qualities of both its parents. It will grow to considerable heights. One of our plants, which we took down to our country home, eventually reached a height of some twelve feet before it was killed by a particularly bitter frost while we were not in residence. Before it died, however, it successfully came through a period when water froze solid in the same room.

It has an almost tree-like habit, growing upwards on a long narrow stem that is unfortunately too weak to support its length. It therefore requires a long stake. The dark green leaves are larger than those of an ivy and smaller than those of a fatsia, though their shape is more reminiscent of the foliage of the latter. A variegated form has creamy margins and stripes in the leaves. The fatshedera is easily propagated by means of stem cuttings taken from the upper, less woody, sections of the main "trunk."

Ficus

From the genus ficus come some of our most popular and most frequently seen house plants. We are apt sometimes to think that house plants are a form of "contemporary" furnishing, yet in one of his later books Dickens complained that a Rubber Plant was to be seen in the front window of every London home. Certainly the Rubber Plant to-day, *Ficus elastica decora*, is still popular. It is a masculine plant, more enjoyed perhaps by men than by women, probably because of its sturdy, tough, muscular appearance.

However the Rubber Plant is by no means the only ficus grown and used as a house plant. Similar in many ways is *F. lyrata*, or the "Fiddle Leaf Fig," whose leaves are lyre-shaped or violin-shaped. Completely different are *F. radicans* and *F. pumila*, each with small leaves and a ground-covering, creeping habit.

The ficus is a member of the *Moraceae*, named after the Morus genus, of which the mulberry is probably the best known member. Ficus actually means fig, and the fig, banyan (with its distinctive long aerial roots) and rubber trees all belong to this group.

The ficus genus is a useful member of the house plant tribe for several reasons. In the first place, it ranges far and wide, as we have seen, and provides us with many plants completely different in appearances and habits. Secondly, nearly all the ficus are easy plants to grow in the home. Thirdly, most ficus will tolerate poor conditions, where there is little light and perhaps even polluted air.

Because of its immense popularity (I suppose the majority of the large number of letters I get, asking for advice about house plants, concern the Rubber Plant) the *F. elastica decora* deserves close attention. It is a carefully cultivated and developed form of the old *F. elastica*, so much improved that the latter is seldom seen to-day, certainly very rarely for sale.

F. elastica decora is an average plant so far as watering is concerned. That is to say, it requires considerable amounts during the spring and summer months while it is growing strongly, but very little indeed during the winter. It should then be allowed to become almost completely dry. One of the most frequent complaints about a Rubber Plant is that the lower leaves have begun to turn yellow and fall off. This is nearly always due to over-watering. Very slight drooping of the normally fairly erect leaves shows that the plant requires water, and is easily remedied.

If a ficus has been given too much water, however, and begins drooping its leaves, then stop watering at once and allow it to have up to a month's convalescence with no food and no water. Towards the end of this time, water lightly, and gradually increase the amounts given until it once again takes its full ration.

The plants will live quite happily in a dark spot in the house, but the leaves will become a slightly lighter tone of green, and the fascinating red sheath containing the emergent leaf will again be pale and less interesting. A light position is therefore better for the plant, but it must never be placed in direct sunlight except for brief periods. As one might imagine with such a stolid plant, it does not like to be disturbed. It likes to stay in one position in the home, to enjoy an even temperature, and to be clear of direct draughts, cold or hot.

Because it has such large leaves the ficus sometimes collects a great deal of dust. This not only detracts from the appearance of the plant; it also hinders its growth. The leaf pores, or stomata, require to be clean in order to breathe properly, and it is therefore helpful once a month or so to wipe the leaves gently with a soft cloth or sponge wrung out in tepid water. Never use oil to get a gloss on the leaves. This merely serves to clog the stomata more dangerously. Use instead a mild milk and water mixture, or a solution of the white oil emulsion "Volck," which has already been mentioned.

A ficus will sometimes grow quite tall, too tall in fact for some homes. In this case it is quite possible to lop the top, when new shoots will branch outwards. If this is done, however, or if there has been some accidental injury to the skin or bark, a milky fluid, the latex or rubber, will be exuded. In time the flow will congeal and stop, but whenever possible it should be stopped artificially. A little powdery soil or sand rubbed over the wound will sometimes stop the bleeding. On the other hand, nothing but good can come from applying a plaster such as you might put on your own finger under similar circumstances.

The elastica will grow well in a remarkably small pot so long as it can still absorb moisture and food. If it obviously needs re-potting, do this in late spring or early summer, so that the plant can spread its roots into the new soil before the winter sets in and all growth is halted. Use John Innes Potting Compost No. 2. As a rough guide, it can be said that in a five-inch pot or 48 a *F. elastica decora* will normally grow happily to some $2\frac{1}{2}$ feet, and will grow two feet taller in each additional inch of pot diameter.

There is a *F. elastica variegata*, but for some reason the variegated form of the Rubber Plant has come to be known as *F. elastica var. doescheri*. It is very pleasant, with a creamy golden variegation in the leaves, which are otherwise very similar to those of *F. elastica*, and a dainty pink flush in the immature foliage. It is, however, rather more delicate. It likes a warmer temperature and more light. It also has a slight tendency to brown at the edges if it is not enjoying the treatment it is getting.

The other large growing ficus that is useful to us as a house plant is *F. lyrata*, the "Fiddle Leaf Fig." The leaves here have a very short stalk, so that they seem almost not to be there. Growing from this stalk, the leaf swells outwards, then inwards again and finally outwards

Saintpaulia Pink Harmony

Philodendron melanochryson and P. ilsemanii

Monstera deliciosa

Euphorbia pulcherrima (poinsettia)

more generously, so that the leaves do really resemble the body of a violin. The main stem or trunk of the plant is thick and sturdy, and the leaves are tough, glossy, quite heavily veined and sometimes slightly curled at the edges. They are quite long, seldom less than nine inches and often up to twelve. The green is lighter than that of the elastica. Once again it is fairly tough and will stand some shade and some cool conditions, but it grows much better if kept fairly warm. It does not like draughts, particularly of warm air, and will soon shed its leaves if subjected to them.

F. radicans is quite different. It is a creeper with small leaves, and is normally available trained up a cane. It is usually seen in its variegated form. It is quite attractive, but difficult to grow, and is not seen very much these days. It likes warmth and humidity, more than is normally available for it, and cannot stand ever being dry at the roots. Winter is a trying time for it in our cool homes, and it is consequently not an entirely satisfactory house plant for us.

Perhaps a little easier to grow is another creeping fig, *F. pumila*. Its leaves are a dark green, very small and so lavishly produced that the thin wiry stems are seldom to be seen. The plant is surprisingly hardy, and in some places will grow out of doors. On the other hand it must never be allowed to dry out, and for this reason it is not completely successful. The root ball must always be moist, even in winter, and although this gives opportunities to the over-waterers even they sometimes fail in their zeal. In a greenhouse, pumila will grow over the soil, staging and wall and almost take the place over under some conditions. It loves the dark.

The only other ficus which should be mentioned in these necessarily general pages is *benjamina*. Once again this bears little resemblance to any others in the same tribe.

It grows to make a delicate weeping tree with small drooping leaves. It is a little difficult to care for, as it likes to be kept warm and well watered. In the absence of conditions it enjoys it is apt to sulk and drop its leaves.

If we come to discuss the propagation of any of the ficus we frequently run into trouble, as a greater degree of bottom heat is necessary than we can normally give. The much loved Rubber Plant, however, can quite easily be increased by means of air layering. At a spot on the main stem not less than nine inches and not more than eighteen inches from the growing tip, remove the bark in a half-inch circle. Wrap around this spot on the stem a good ball of damp sphagnum moss, and tie it securely in place with string. Over this ball tie some plastic sheeting so that it is airtight. In a matter of a few weeks roots will grow into the moss. Then cut away the whole of the tip below this point and pot up the new plant, for that is actually what it will be.

Hedera

The hedera or ivy has become almost synonymous with house plants. This is because the ivies are so numerous, and because they happily live under conditions which kill almost everything else that grows. But although the ivies are so numerous, they are all of exactly the same character and type, being different only in minor degrees of leaf coloration, size and shape. I think I am correct in saying, however, that it was the ivies which started the house plant fashion as we know it to-day in this country.

Plants in the home have been a part of civilised life for thousands of years, but it was only in the mid or late forties that that wonderful personality Constance Spry realised their potential, and went to Thomas Rochford to ask him to grow some special ivies for her. Sparked off by this request, Tom Rochford (to whom we all owe more than we can ever repay) investigated further, mainly in Scandinavia, and began to grow not only ivies but some other house plants too. Since then he has never looked back, and because of his vigorous, progressive outlook, he now runs the largest house plant nursery in the world, acres and acres of greenhouses all within a few miles of the smoke and grime of London.

To return to our ivies. The hedera is a member of the *araliaceae*, a family from which many members have been plucked by the confusion of modern horticultural nomenclature and dropped willy-nilly into several different categories. The ivies abound in number, tolerate the most unpleasant conditions, grow in any soil, and confine themselves in tiny pots. Most of the ivies have small leaves, although some have large and dramatic ones. Nearly all are self-branching, producing shoots from almost every leaf joint when the growing tip has been pinched out, a habit which places it much above the normal wild ivy.

I have heard people complain on being charged five shillings for an ivy plant, saying that they could get hundreds of ivies from their own garden plants. I cannot emphasise too strongly that there is all the difference in the world between wild varieties and cultivated hybrids. Again I must point out that garden varieties are (with very few exceptions) not the same as pot-grown. Many of the ivy plants that one grows indoors will never successfully grow in the garden, except during the spring and summer. Some, however, will, and even the slightly tender *Hedera canariensis* will grow out of doors if it is introduced to the larger world gently. Against an east wall of our Gloucestershire cottage a *Hedera canariensis* is growing very well (apart from the occasional nibbles it gets from passing sheep), and this was at one time a coddled pot plant growing with the protection and comfort of roof, walls, shielded light and a comfortable degree of heating.

67

One of our best ivies, however, is one which we took to the country from London, and which survived through a very cold spell while we were away. In the summer, in order to bring it round and give it a better chance of future life, we planted the pot in a sheltered and slightly shaded place in the garden. There it was left until the autumn, and then re-potted in pure sand in a huge wine crock. It has lived in this wine crock for four or five years, and now climbs eight feet to the ceiling and in places two feet or more through. It receives no special attention, although it is fed regularly during the spring and summer and watered less frequently during the colder months. It has formed a solid column of living green and encourages many of our visitors to take up growing ivies.

I do not intend here to go into great detail about the many varieties of hedera that are normally available to us. Perhaps if I point out the many differences between some of the varieties and their hybrids, this will be sufficient to indicate the wide choice that is available to us.

Hedera helix is the name of our common wild ivy. The suffix helix is a Latin word meaning snail, and indicates that the stem of the ivy curls or twines its way around the tree trunk or other object which impedes its growth. The ivy is possessed of hair-like aerial roots with which it clings to a tree stump or a wall, and from which it draws sustenance to help its further growth. As a general rule the aerial roots are still visible on the stem of house plant ivies, but not having anything to which they can cling and receiving little in the way of moisture or aerial humidity, the roots are of little significance indoors. Most ivies are normally available to us already trained up a cane some two feet or so in length. We can either continue their upward growth along these or taller canes, or we can release the trails and train them on other supports, or let them trail elegantly downwards.

Although in America the hedera is generally known as the English ivy, some of our own better known hybrids bear the names of American cities. *Hedera helix Pittsburgh* for example, was perhaps the first of the self-branching ivies to be introduced into this country. It has triangular-shaped leaves, one inch long and with five lobes. Close on its heels was *H. h. Chicago*, which has leaves nearly as large. The variegated form of Chicago, which tends to revert to its original green, has been more or less supplanted by *H. h. harald*. Other varieties include: the tiny-leafed *H. h. minima* and *H. h. Maple Queen*, and *H. h. Little Diamond* with its tiny grey-green or cream leaves. Maple Queen is probably the best of these, as it grows strongly and makes few demands.

H. h. glacier has grey-green, cream-margined foliage which varies considerably in size. Some leaves may be two inches in length and width in their widest portion and others may be no more than half this size. Not strictly self-branching, glacier nevertheless produces sufficient side-shoots to make a large and bushy plant. One that I possess is some six feet in height and a foot through at the base.

Immediate attention was gained by *H. h. Green Ripple* when it was first introduced a few years ago. It has five-lobed two-inch leaves, of a light green which darkens with age. Quite different is *H. h. cristata* with its curled and crumpled leaf edges. One of my own favourites is *H. h. Ravenholst*, which will grow very large indeed, and which has enormous glossy green leaves. If these are kept sponged and clean the plant is a handsome one indeed.

The variegated ivies depend mainly upon *Hedera canariensis*, which comes from the Canary Islands. The varieties offered have green, grey and cream leaves fairly large in size. The plants are perhaps a little more tender than the general run of ivies, requiring careful watering if they are to retain their foliage for long periods. Although they are not quick growers, with a modicum of care they can be kept for some years, and then will develop into large and attractive plants.

Maranta

The maranta is a member of the *Marantaceae*, which family includes the gingers and arrowroot, among many others. In the family are a number of useful and decorative house plants, which are well worth growing in spite of the somewhat delicate nature of most of them. The marantas like to be warm and humid, and in fact the warmer and more humid their conditions the better they will grow. They do not like sunlight, dry soil, draughts or over-damp roots. Most of them lift their leaves upwards at night, which has resulted in their being given the common name of "Prayer Plant."

Maranta leuconeura is named after two Greek words which suggest that the leaves are veined with white. The two varieties most frequently seen are *kerchoveana* and *massangeana*. Kerchoveana has oval leaves, four or five inches long and nearly as wide, of a light green colour darkening when they are mature, and with reddish blotches between the veins. Its leaves are almost velvety in appearance. Massangeana is rather more spreading in habit, and has vivid white veins on its leaves and a less striking blotch between the veins. The undersides of the leaves are reddish brown in colour. Both varieties grow strongly and require heavier feeding than is normal in the summer months, and more frequent re-potting. Re-potting should be carried out in late spring.

In view of their liking for warm and humid conditions, marantas are best kept with their pots plunged in moist peat or some other moisture retentive material. They enjoy an occasional steam bath. This is usually given to them by standing the pot inside a slightly larger water receptacle which in turn stands in the centre of an even larger basin. If the basin receives an inch or two of hot but not boiling water, the steam will rise and surround the plant to the benefit of its foliage.

New plants can be obtained by division of the creeping underground stem or rhizome. This should be done in the spring or a little earlier.

Monstera

The *Monstera deliciosa* is probably my own favourite among house plants. It has large leaves of a dark glossy green, a foot or more in length and nearly as wide. These leaves are slashed and holed outwards from the mid-rib, giving the plants a most strange and fantastic appearance. The plant in my own office is already some ten feet high, and I have a vivid recollection of seeing one growing in a Belgian bistro which extended from its pot to just below the ceiling, and then some 20 feet along the wall. This suggests with some certainty that the plant is an easy one to grow, but it hints also that unless a careful control is kept on it, the monstera might very well outgrow its position in the average small home.

The plant is an aroid, and has thick aerial roots growing from its main stems. Our aim should be to train these down into the soil again, but this is obviously an impossibility under normal conditions. If on the other hand the plant can be grown up a stout stake, or moss-wrapped can, then the roots will grow into or cling on to this, and if moistened occasionally the roots will subtract this nourishment and pass it to the upper shoots of the plant.

Although I have never yet been able to bring a monstera to flower or fruit, I have seen several in this condition in greenhouses and have bought the fruit, which is occasionally obtainable in the greengrocery departments of some of our more opulent stores. It is roughly the size of a sweet-corn cob and in appearance much like a tightly packed green pine cone. The flesh is soft and succulent, with a flavour reminiscent of a cross between pineapple and banana.

The monstera likes plenty of water in summer, and little in winter. Like so many large plants it enjoys feeling at home. In other words, once it is placed in position in the home it will settle down, and if too frequently moved, so that it receives different intensities of light and warmth, it will begin to feel uncomfortable and will turn yellow or brown at the leaf edges. Again, as in the case with all large-leafed plants, the foliage should be kept clean. Dust settles rapidly on them. An occasional spray of tepid water helps to keep them clean, but as this is not practicable in most homes, it is usually better to sponge the leaves very gently with clean water or with a mixture of water and milk.

The plant grows so prolifically that it is necessary to support it at all stages. It can be trained up a stout cane, or supported by means of training wires or string firmly tied to the wall.

Fairly recently a variegated form of monstera has been introduced in this country. The leaves are much the same in shape but slightly paler in colour, with gold and cream blotches and flecks.

The easiest way of propagating a monstera is by means of a top cutting. This will root fairly easily under normal conditions in a light well-drained soil mixture. Leaf joint cuttings and seeds can also be used for propagation, but as they require fairly high degrees of heat, this is more a matter for the specialist.

Nidularium

I indulged in a slight hesitation before including this

bromeliad in this book of house plants. The hesitation was due in no way to any lack of belief in the nidularium as a house plant, but rather to doubt as to whether or not it was of sufficient importance and whether it could be easily enough obtained. My decision was that it is important enough, but my research into its availability was less promising. I can only say that if you are determined to obtain a specimen then you must insist that your supplier get one for you. He can do this through the wholesale trade, but he may have to search and he (and you) may have to wait.

The nidularium is one of those familiar bromeliads which form a leaf rosette or "vase", which is normally kept topped up with water. While some similar plants are largely popular because of the brilliant flower thrown up from the centre of this rosette, the nidularium lets us down and gives birth to some insignificant greenish-white or lilac flowers which hardly show above the water. What makes the plant attractive, however, is its foliage.

Nidularium innocentii has strap-like leaves about twelve inches in length and about two inches wide. They are basically a dark green in colour, with reddish purple flecks on the top and a deep, dark red on the underside. When the flowers appear, the leaves in the centre of the rosette change colour and take on a vivid scarlet hue, fascinating and unusual to see.

The plant is an easy one to keep as long as temperatures do not fall below what one would regard as normally comfortable. The central vase should always be kept with a little water in it, but otherwise the plant seldom requires much moisture. The soil it grows in should be well drained. Nidularium can be reproduced by means of offsets, but these generally like a certain amount of heat before they can be induced to send out roots.

Peperomia

The peperomia is a genus of the *piperaceae*, a family containing the producer of domestic or culinary pepper, *Piper nigrum*. Of the 400 or so species of peperomia less than a dozen are really suited to room culture, but these, because of their neat habit of growth, their ease of culture, and their ornamental nature, are particularly fitted to be called house plants.

All the peperomias have a small and confined root, which means that they can be grown in small pots with little fear of the plants becoming pot-bound. They are all comparatively small and compact, and all have similar flowers, in appearance something like a rat's tail, which are composed of dozens of tiny flowers.

Where peperomias differ one from another is in their foliage. Most varieties have a thick and chunky leaf, almost succulent in appearance, which rightly suggests that the plant can exist for some time with meagre supplies of moisture. The plants in fact require comparatively little water, and in the cold season should be allowed to live in an almost dry state. If by following this rule the leaves are seen to shrink and shrivel, then an application of water, preferably tepid, will fatten them up very quickly and seldom will the plant itself come to any real harm.

Peperomia caperata is a small plant, producing a mass of tiny, corrugated, heart-shaped leaves, dark green on top, and green and purple underneath. The flower spikes are white and sometimes branch like a snake's tongue at the tip.

With smooth leaves, thick and chunky, *P. argyreia* grows to eight or nine inches in height. The leaves are striped dark green and silver, almost metallic in appearance. This is a most striking plant, frequently still sold under the old name of *P. sandersii*.

Great, thick, leathery leaves are possessed by *P. obtusifolia*, one of the toughest of the peperomias. The plant grows a foot or so tall, and the leaves are about four inches long and two inches wide, a dark green in colour with a purple edge. The stems are a reddish-purple. Obtusifolia requires very little water and will take almost any punishment except over-watering.

One of the best known forms of peperomia is known as *P. magnoliaefolia* because of a reputed similarity to the leaves of the magnolia. The similarity is not very striking, but it can just be seen. The leaves are chunky in shape, mainly green and cream in colour and about two inches long. It makes a pleasant though not very dramatic plant, and is quite easy to keep for long periods in the home.

Similar in some ways to magnoliaefolia is *P. glabella*, another favourite. This one is really a trailer, and will become somewhat straggly and elongated unless the trails are pinched out at their ends occasionally. Once again the leaves are mainly green and cream, borne on pinkish stems. Glabella does not like too much water, and will show its dislike of this treatment by setting up stem rot, which will quickly spread.

P. hederaefolia has crinkled and corrugated leaves similar in some respects to caperata but nearly twice as large. Its colours are mainly grey and green.

To sum up on this rather large family of house plants, one might say that all the peperomias are valuable, engaging little plants which make few demands as long as they are not over-watered. The rat-tail flowers, rising on stalks above the leaves, are always interesting.

Philodendron

If we were limited to one tribe of house plants we could choose philodendrons, and still fill our home with a large range of easy to grow, fascinating and dramatic forms of indoor decoration. The philodendrons are aroids and many of them are climbers. The name philodendron in fact comes from the Greek meaning "tree lover," and in their native home of South America many climb up jungle trees or spread over rocks and hillsides. Many varieties have aerial roots, which in the home can either be utilised to provide additional sustenance to the upper reaches of the plant, or can be ignored without doing any real harm to it.

Some commercial growers of philodendrons send them out from their nurseries with their aerial roots trained on to a piece of bark, piece of wood or a cane well-covered with sphagnum moss. The aerial roots will grow on to or into these materials if they are kept moist. Naturally cork bark or wood will absorb very little moisture, and in warm weather may need to be sprayed at least once a day. Even if this aid to growth has not been provided by the grower (it takes time and material) then it is advantageous to provide it yourself. On the other hand it is not necessary, and any aerial roots your plant may have or may produce can either be ignored completely, or may be pruned away if they are considered to be unsightly. The plant may not do quite so well but it will certainly suffer no mortal wound.

One of the originals among house plants in this country was *Philodendron scandens*, a climber with green, heart-shaped leaves. At one time it was so popular that it achieved the name of "Bathroom Plant." This appeared to be because many housewives possessed more than one plant, either given or bought and in order to spread them around the house one was relegated to the bathroom. Certainly the bathroom (as long as it is heated) is a splendid place for many house plants. It is a naturally humid room and frequently provides better conditions for house plants than are found in other parts of the house. *P. scandens* achieved great popularity in its early days and it has never really lost it. This is because it is an attractive plant, easy to grow and highly decorative. Although it is strictly a climber and will either climb or trail quite happily, it sometimes becomes straggly. In this case it will branch easily and make a much more stocky plant if the growing tips are pinched out to encourage side shoots. Its aerial roots are not obtrusive and if ignored will hardly be noticed. On the other hand if they are actively encouraged by means of a moss-covered pole, they will develop and catch hold of the moist stake.

When it was first introduced, we were sent a plant of *P. melanochrysum*. We were told that it was rather tender and could not really be expected to live for very long under home conditions. We were so enchanted with the plant that we were determined to enjoy its brief life, and thus we potted it up in a mixed group in a huge old Victorian foot bath. It lasted for months and months, perhaps not in its pristine state but certainly maintaining much of its original beauty. The leaves are like an elongated arrow-head, and appear to be made of a fine, dark green velvet. As with some velvets, the sheen of the tiny hairs of which it is composed appears to change colour in different lights, and the leaves of melanochrysum appear sometimes to be dark green, sometimes almost black, but always overlaid with a sheen of fine gold. This really is a most beautiful plant and it seems a great pity that it is not more readily available in our shops and markets. The reason for its scarcity is simply that it is difficult to grow well or for long periods, and growers consequently hesitate to put it on the market lest they be blamed for its shortcomings. On the other hand, if you insist, your supplier of house plants will almost certainly be able to obtain one for you, and judging from my own experience, I believe that you will find it not so difficult a plant to care for as it is reputed to be.

A rare non-climber among the philodendrons is *P.*

bipinnatifidum. The explanation of the name is somewhat complex and confusing, so we shall say here merely that the leaves are more or less round, about a foot or more in diameter, and slashed towards the centre so that they are almost like a many-fingered hand. The leaves come out from a central point on long stems, so that although the plant is not a climber it is still quite large. It cannot, however, be pruned to make it branch out. The leaves are the usual glossy green, and the plant is extremely effective as decoration. It is quite easy to grow, liking always to be kept slightly moist but hating over-watering. As might be expected it is propagated only by seed.

On a dressing table in my bedroom is a plant of *P. erubescens.* It is a new hybrid which has been given the name "Burgundy." This is reasonable enough, for although the leaves are generally a dark and glossy green, they are edged with a dark red, and the underside is generally burgundy coloured with a paler green showing through. The stems bearing the leaves are also burgundy coloured. The leaves are arrow shaped, nearly a foot in length. One or two of them have small holes, almost like nostrils, in the very apex or point of the leaf. A further curiosity about this plant is that during the warmer months I have frequently noticed that its leaves have perspired. Small drops of water have appeared at the edges and have dripped slowly down to the leaf points. In our own plant the aerial roots, which are produced at each leaf joint, are left to fend for themselves.

Philodendron elegans is similar in some respects to bipinnatifidum in its foliage, though the fingers are more distinct and separated. It is, however, a climber and produces characteristic aerial roots. The effect of the deeply incised leaves is, indeed, elegant, but because the leaves are large, usually well over a foot in length, they sometimes get a little floppy, and together with the exposed aerial roots the plant as a whole can sometimes look a little like a tangled skein of knitting wool.

One of the comparatively few philodendrons which is variegated is *ilsemannii*, which is seldom seen for sale, probably because it is a slow grower and so not an economic proposition. It is nevertheless extremely attractive and well worth obtaining. The six to eight inch arrow-shaped leaves begin as a light pink and gradually turn dark green. The whitish speckles and blotches are maintained during this change of colour, and the leaves eventually become a mottled cream and green, quite unlike any of the other philodendrons. Apart from being a slow grower it also has a need for more light than most others of the same family. This follows the normal rule that variegated plants require light in order to maintain their colour.

Two philodendrons so similar that fairly close examination is necessary to separate them are *P. imbe* and *P. sagittifolium*. Both have long, narrow, arrow-head leaves of dark green, and both are climbers. Imbe is recognised by purple spots on stems and petioles. It is also more of a rampant grower and will sometimes grow too large for modern rooms. Sagittifolium's leaves are a little smaller, and neither its stems nor its petioles have the reddish purple spots of imbe. Besides being a slower grower, sagittifolium will tolerate more difficult conditions, particularly lack of heat.

There are several other philodendrons which could be mentioned, but no others are at present easily obtained, and some are difficult to keep. The family is, however, a most fascinating and useful one, and we can expect to see several further species introduced in years to come.

Pilea

Although not perhaps of great importance in the houseplant world, the pileas produce one or two interesting and attractive little plants. The pilea, in fact, belongs to the *Urticaceae*, or nettle family, to which also belongs the hop vine used in brewing.

The best-known and most beautiful of the house plant pileas is *P. cadieri*, popular because of its three inch, dark green, oval leaves. Their green is relieved by regular patches of silver spaced down the midrib and separated by the veins. The plant is a quick grower, and the growing tips should be pinched out regularly to produce a nice bushy shape rather than a straggly appearance. It accepts cool conditions quite well.

The other pilea is sold mainly as a curiosity, and largely for children. It is *P. muscosa*, which is almost fern-like in appearance. The stems are densely covered with rosettes of minute green leaves, in the centre of which can just be seen the equally tiny flowers. These flowers produce quantities of dusty pollen, and when the plant is tapped with a pencil it will give off what appears to be a puff of smoke. This has given it the name of "Artillery Plant" and a secure place in the hearts of many children.

Both pileas are easy to grow, and make no special demands. They can be propagated by means of cuttings or division, and root readily.

Platycerium

Although strictly a fern, *Platycerium bifurcatum* has earned its place here through its popularity and its fitness as a house plant. It is known as the "Stag's Horn Fern" because of the characteristic shape of the large, grey-green fronds. Even the Greek name gives a clue to the appearance of the plant: *platys*, broad and *keras*, horn.

This fern is an epiphyte, and grows best on a block of wood or cork hung on a wall. A minimum of sphagnum moss and peat are all it requires for its sustenance. As it is

Peperomia obtusifolia

Aphelandra Saffron Spike

*Dracaena bruanti, D. sanderiana
and D. terminalis*

Sansevieria trifasciata

Group of opuntias

Spathiphyllum wallisii

difficult to water the plant when hung on a living-room wall, it is fortunate that it accepts eagerly the limited amount of water we can safely give it. The best method of handling is to allow the plant to stay in its position until the fronds begin to get soft and drooping. Then the roots and block of wood should be soaked thoroughly in water, set aside to drain, and when dry enough replaced on the wall.

It can, of course, be grown perfectly well in a pot like any other plant, but it really looks best when viewed from below. In a high position in a greenhouse they obviously get plenty of light. This they need, and it is therefore necessary to make sure that if they are hung on a wall in a living-room they will still get plenty of light, for this position is sometimes comparatively dark.

Platycerium bifurcatum is usually propagated by offsets, which sometimes appear on larger and more mature plants. The process of propagating from spores is a lengthy one and not generally for the amateur.

Plectranthus

For some reason the plectranthus seems to be ignored by nearly all authorities on house plants. It is seldom written about, and seldom listed by house plant growers. This is surprising, for it makes a splendid decoration in the home, is easily grown and roots almost immediately from stem cuttings.

The plectranthus is a member of the *labiatae*, a genus of nearly 100 species of herbs and shrubs native to many parts of the tropical and sub-tropical world. The varieties most suitable for house plants are *P. fruiticosus* and *P. oertendahlii*.

P. fruticosus has glossy green leaves shaped like a very fat heart, almost circular, and varying in size from one to almost three inches in diameter. From a stem cutting a couple of inches long one can obtain in a single season great trails three feet or more in length, and if the growing tip is pinched out then it will branch attractively. The leaves vary considerably in colour, depending on the feeding of the plant and the amount of light it receives. They can be a deep dark glossy green with a paler underside, or a light green on both sides.

A rather hairy leaf of much the same shape, with a purple underside, is produced by *P. oertendahlii*. It has exactly the same tolerant habit of growth as fruticosus. Both plants like to be moist at the roots and will flag when they are dry. Little harm seems to come to them if they are left for considerable periods, however, and a drink will freshen them up in a matter of a few hours. They will stand cool conditions quite well and will live happily in a draught.

The plant that we first possessed some years ago has now become at least half a dozen, which we grow easily both in London and in the country, and we have seen further cuttings in the homes of friends, all of which appear to be flourishing. The plant looks particularly pleasant set high in a room so that the trails hang prettily downwards.

We sometimes break off a piece of a growing tip and insert it in a pot of well-drained soil, and sometimes we merely place a cutting in a small container of plain water, where we can see the roots developing in a matter of days.

Rhoicissus

In earlier pages I have mentioned the inexplicable difficulty I have in keeping a *Cissus antarctica* in good condition for a long time. Very similar in many ways to the cissus is the *Rhoicissus rhomboidea*, yet this is reputed to be slightly more delicate and I can keep it indefinitely! Don't ask me to explain this—I merely report it.

Another vine, the rhoicissus, known as "Grape Ivy," is

in fact related to the cissus, and shows its difference mainly by the three-part leaves. These leaves are a dark green and slightly toothed. When they first appear and begin to grow they are soft, downy, and of a tan or cinnamon colour.

The rhoicissus, in spite of its difficult name, has been one of the standard house plants in the shops and in our homes for many years now. This is because it has a pleasant appearance and is easy to look after. It is a climber of course, but it will also trail downwards very attractively. It grows quickly and easily, will accept light or shade, and does not really mind whether the temperature is warm or cool. It will tolerate a lot of variation in the watering it receives. About its only real dislike is draughts. While it will object to hot air driven from a fan-operated electric fire, for example, it will nevertheless accept a light breeze from a window on a summer day.

The meaning in Greek of the prefix *rhoia* is pomegranate, and a possible explanation of this lies in the fruit. I do not think that it is normally likely that a rhoicissus will produce its berries except under ideal greenhouse conditions, and in fact I have never even seen a rhoicissus in berry, but the fruits are said to have from one to four seeds in them. This probably explains the name. They are edible, by the way, in case any reader should confound me and produce a fruiting plant.

Sansevieria

Another of our most popular house plants is the sansevieria. It has achieved its popularity for several reasons: its tolerance of home conditions, its strange appearance, and its popular name. A really good popular name, one which catches the imagination, does a great deal to "sell" a plant. Witness, for example, "Stag's Horn Fern,"

"India Rubber Plant," "Dumb Cane" and the name for sansevieria, "Mother-in-Law's Tongue." The name, of course, comes from the long, spear-like and sharply pointed leaves.

Sansevieria trifasciata Laurentii is the variety most frequently seen. It produces leaves 18 inches or more in length, of a dark green mottled and striped with grey and yellow. There is a fine yellow stripe running round the edges of the leaves. With its fleshy leaves, the plant can live for considerable periods with little or no water, and in fact an excess of moisture at the roots is about the only thing that will kill it, particularly if this excess is given during the cold months of winter.

This tolerance of dry conditions led us in our first experiences of the sansevieria to keep our plants rather too dry. They appeared to flourish less than they should, and at the same time we found that the plants were top-heavy and were constantly being knocked over. For some reason or other we began giving them rather more water during the summer months, and soon found we had cured both troubles. The leaves flourished and multiplied, and because of the additional weight of water in the pot at the base of the plants, they were knocked over less frequently. This is still a danger, however, with the sansevieria, and so we always keep our plants now inside another and heavier container, which keeps them steady.

The sansevieria will increase itself quickly and regularly from its creeping rhizome rootstock if it likes the treatment it is receiving. As might be expected, the larger the pot the greater the concentration of new plants, but it is surprising how much will grow in a small pot. It is also surprising how tall the spears will grow given good treatment. It is usually said that they will grow no more than a maximum of two feet or so in a pot, but some of our own specimens are near the three foot mark. If they are planted in a larger trough or a tub they will grow even larger, and cover a considerable area in a couple of years.

Propagation is simple, the best way being by division of the rhizome. The stems themselves will root if cut into sections two or three inches long, and put into a slightly heavier soil than is enjoyed by most house plants. But if the plants are grown from these cuttings they will be found to have lost the attractive gold stripes that are a feature of *S. t. Laurentii*. The plant reverts, in fact, to the original of the variety and becomes merely *Sansevieria trifasciata*.

Saxifraga

So easy to grow that it reproduces itself almost embarrass-ingly is *Saxifraga sarmentosa*. This has a number of popular names: "Mother of Thousands," "Aaron's Beard," "Roving Sailor" and "Strawberry Geranium." In some ways it is in fact very like a strawberry, for it pro-duces large numbers of runners. Attached to the mother plant are long hair-like shoots with a new young plant growing at the end. The leaves are marbled reddish purple with a fine down on them.

The saxifraga looks particularly attractive placed so that the runners can hang downwards. They are pro-duced in such quantity that they look almost like straggly hair. The plant grows easily and very freely in the warmer months of the year. When it is growing strongly it likes plenty of water, but it will revive at once in water after a period of drought.

During the summer months it should be given a regular dose of fertiliser, for in addition to the production of its many stolons it also raises long arching stems which carry pretty little pink flowers. It will tolerate quite cool conditions, but enjoys plenty of light though not bright sunlight. We have found ourselves that a particularly suitable position is in a north-facing window.

The plant is propagated like a strawberry, by placing one of the baby plants at the end of a stolon on to a pot of good soil. It quickly makes roots, and the stolon can then be cut. After a year or two, so quickly does *S. sarmentosa* reproduce itself that the surface of the pot will be covered and matted with young plants. These should be divided in order to obtain really good specimens.

Scindapsus

Similar in many respects to *Philodendron scandens* is *Scindapsus aureus*. It has the same roughly heart-shaped leaf, the same climbing habit, and even the same treatment should be given to it. It has achieved considerable popularity, and from personal observation I should say that some plant owners confuse one with the other. There are several varieties of *S. aureus*.

The leaves are green, heavily flecked and splashed with butter yellow. It is normally bought with the growing shoots loosely clipped to a central cane. Less frequently the shoots are already growing on to a moss-covered support, a block of wood or cork bark, and if in fact you see a plant like this, buy it. The aerial roots grow into a support of this nature, and the plant produces much better, bigger and more brightly coloured foliage. In time the plant will outgrow its support, and to prevent it getting leggy and straggling it is helpful to pinch out the growing tip to help it shoot afresh. As a variegated plant it likes plenty of light, but direct sunlight should be avoided. The leaves sometimes "burn" with little brown patches. Indeed one of the difficulties of this plant is the fact that it tends to brown at the edges of the leaves if it is in a draught, if it is too wet, or if it is bruised.

Marble Queen is probably the best-known of the cultivars of *Scindapsus aureus*. The leaves are creamy

86

white in colour. A further cultivar is *Golden Queen,* with yellow predominating.

Cuttings can be taken from these plants in order to propagate them, but as they tend to revert to the original green this should be done carefully.

Spathiphyllum

The name of this plant suggests that the spathe or bract enclosing the flower is in appearance similar to the leaf. The plant is an aroid and is grown mainly for its flower, which is similar to the wild British arum commonly known as the "Lords and Ladies" or "Jack in the Pulpit." The variety usually found is *S. wallisii,* which has dark green spear-shaped leaves which are very glossy and quite attractive in themselves. The flower bract is white, surrounding a cream-coloured spike of flower.

The spathiphyllum enjoys fairly warm conditions and does not like the somewhat varying temperatures of our winter rooms. It also likes a fairly high degree of humidity. In the summer the roots should be constantly moist, and the plant will respond to an occasional spraying with clean water at room temperature. It will live happily away from bright light. The flowers, which are few, will nevertheless live for some weeks under good conditions. Propagation is by division of the roots. Some degree of heat and humidity is helpful during propagation.

Syngonium

Popularly known as the "Goose Foot Plant," because of the shape of its three-lobed leaves, *Syngonium vellozianum* is an attractive and easily grown aroid. It has dark green leaves, and is a climber which grows easily up a cane or other support. Although it produces aerial roots, they are rather exceptional in being of modest size and of little real importance. The plant tends to become somewhat straggly if it grows too tall, and it is therefore helpful to pinch out the growing stem to encourage the plant to shoot.

Although these tropical American shrubs enjoy a warm moist atmosphere, they are tolerant of cooler, dryer conditions and will accept a fairly dark corner in which to grow. They will take in fact a considerable degree of neglect, although admittedly in these conditions they lose something of their charm.

Tetrastigma

Some years ago when we occupied premises with a rather low ceiling, we grew a tetrastigma against a room division and remarked on how easy a plant it was to grow. It was most vigorous, reaching the ceiling in a very short time. Eventually the main stem snapped and broke because it outgrew its own strength. We have recently gained another tetrastigma, and this time we are making sure that it is allowed plenty of room for growth, and that its considerable weight is properly supported.

A common name given to *Tetrastigma voinierianum* is the "Chestnut Vine," probably because the foliage is similar in some ways to that of a horse chestnut tree. The leaves are large, fleshy, and in their young state covered with a soft fluff or down, much as a horse chestnut's are when they are forced indoors.

In its natural home in Asia the tetrastigma climbs up forest trees, twining its tendrils around various stems and twigs and supporting itself in this manner. I have noticed that, grown in the home, the tendrils seem rather more reluctant to curl around a supporting cane than are those of most vines. As the weight of the large leaves is so great, it is vital to keep the growing stems clipped firmly to the cane as it grows upwards. Fortunately new shoots grow easily and quickly, so that if a stem breaks another soon appears in its place.

The plant will grow happily in a room away from direct light, although more light is appreciated during the winter days. The roots should be kept on the moist side, certainly during the summer, but no special degree of humidity is required. As it springs up so quickly, it likes an occasional feed when it is growing fast.

Tillandsia

The genus tillandsia is a bromeliad. It contains upwards of 400 species, of which only one or two are suitable for house plants. The tillandsias, however, are among the very few plants which will grow fairly easily indoors, and produce flowers of breathtaking beauty and exceptionally long life. The two species available to us as house plants, for example, both produce flowers which will begin, develop, and gradually die over a period of from six to ten weeks, and even without the flowers we shall still have a plant of some decorative value.

The genus is named in honour of a Swedish botanist, Elias Tillands, who was also a professor of medicine. It comes from tropical and sub-tropical South America. The flowers grow at the end of a long stem or scape which itself is sometimes beautifully coloured. They appear from the centre of gorgeously coloured bracts, which are mainly in various tints of pink, with flowers usually blue or purple.

T. cyanea has blue flowers. They arise from the centre of a rosette of dark green leaves. At the top of the scape are a series of interleaved pink bracts nearly six inches long containing the blue flowers, which open stage by stage from the bottom upwards. The flowers themselves last only from three days to a week, but as they open gradually upwards and as the inflorescence persists, the whole decorative effect continues for many weeks.

There are several varieties of *T. lindeniana*, named after the Belgian gardener Linden. They have decorative leaves, purple-green, long and arching, as well as flowers. The flower spike is about six inches long at the end of a stem of equal length. The pink bracts last for weeks, and enclose the violet-blue flowers. These have a shorter life, but they open gradually so that they spread their general effect over several weeks.

The tillandsias like to live in a really sunny window where they get plenty of warmth and strong light. Naturally enough, in a position like this they dry out quickly, so that watering during the summer months should be quite lavish. During winter they require less water but should never be allowed to dry out completely. Although they enjoy this light, warmth and water, they will exist without one or the other of them. In this case, however, they will not flourish, and flowering may be delayed. It is helpful during the hot days to give them a daily spray with clean water.

Tillandsias are propagated by suckers, which will appear around the base of a well grown plant, but should be permitted to grow quite large before they are detached and potted up.

Tradescantia

This very popular plant was named after John Tradescant, gardener to Charles I. There were three John Tradescants, father, son and grandson, all of them gardeners, and all of them expert botanists. All are buried in the churchyard of St. Mary's Church at Lambeth Palace in London, official residence to this day of the Archbishop of Canterbury.

Regarding these, as with so many of our house plants, botanically accurate nomenclature is rarely to be found except in more erudite journals, and in order to be practical we must rely on our more popular dictionaries and authorities. *Tradescantia fluminensis* appears to be the accepted name for the form of this plant that is most frequently seen. Popularly known as "Wandering Jew," or "Wandering Sailor," this is one of the spiderworts that we grow in the garden. It is not a climber but a trailer, and though it is generally bought with half a dozen or so short stems growing in a single pot, each of these stems will in a single season grow several feet in length and tumble down over the rim of the pot.

The leaves are an inch or so in length, and may be found with their basic light green striped with silver or gold. They require plenty of light to maintain their colour, and if the plant is kept too long in a dark spot they are apt to revert to a simple dark green. The trails are apt to become overlong, straggly and somewhat bare if permitted to remain without pinching out. Pinched out tops can be inserted into a pot of soil, where they will quickly take root, or can be placed in water where the roots can be watched growing in a matter of only a few days. Some of the silver tradescantias will attain a violet hue if given plenty of light. If this tinge or background colour is required, the easiest way to obtain it is to pinch out the cuttings, which should be potted in good soil in a *new* pot. They should be watered in thoroughly, and the pot should then be allowed to become almost completely dry. Dryish conditions should be maintained, with plenty of light, in order to retain the violet tinge in the leaves.

If a plant has been kept for some time it may produce tiny white flowers. This indicates that it is reaching the end of its life. The best thing to do under these conditions is to take further cuttings from the plant and then do away with it completely.

T. blossfeldiana has rather larger leaves, which are olive green and slightly hairy. There is a purplish tinge on the undersides of the leaves and sometimes in stripes along the top. All these tradescantias are particularly attractive when grown so that their trails will hang downwards. All of them should be pinched out regularly to keep the leaves growing richly, and all should be allowed plenty of light. On the other hand *T. regina* grows directly on a single stem with much longer leaves, up to six inches in length, growing alternatively off the main stem. They are a greyish-green with a vivid purple underside.

Although all these tradescantias grow quite easily under normal house conditions, they will do even better in a greenhouse where they get the warmth, humidity and light that they prefer. They are frequently to be seen growing underneath a staging, where they will spread rampantly unless kept in check. It cannot too strongly be emphasised that due to their luxuriant habit of growth, they require regular pinching out at the growing tips to keep them attractive and under control.

Vriesia

Not as well-known as it deserves to be, but growing gradually in popularity and assured in the future of a significant place in the house plant world, is the vriesia, another bromeliad which has habits similar in some ways to those of the aechmea, cryptanthus, nidularium and tillandsia.

As with so many plants, it grows in the form of a rosette carrying a central stem of flowers from its centre or "vase." It is distinguished largely by its wide leaves and its small flowers. The leaves of some varieties, however, are particularly gorgeously coloured. Without exception, so far as the house plant varieties are concerned, the flowers are yellow in colour.

The easiest and finest species is *Vriesia splendens*,

which has dark green leaves about a foot long and about three inches wide, green above and a purple brown below with reddish purple bands. When the flowering stem begins to emerge the leaves tend to lose their brighter colouring. An exception to the general rule, the flower scape here is as much as a foot long and two inches wide. The bracts are scarlet, retaining their colour for a couple of months, with yellow flowers of a brief life emerging from them.

V. fenestralis has particularly interesting leaves a foot or more in length, broad, arched, and pale green, with purple coloured flecks and blotchings tinted green, brown and red. The flowers in this case are a greenish yellow, emerging from green bracts. However, the flowers in this variety are of considerably less interest than the superb foliage. Again mainly distinguished for its leaves, which are a dark green with black bands, *V. hieroglyphica* produces yellow flowers emerging from yellow bracts. *V. carinata* is much smaller than the other species, with six-inch green leaves, and red and yellow bracts producing yellow flowers which have a brief 24-hour life.

Zebrina

The zebrina is sometimes mistaken for a tradescantia, for it is similar in appearance and habit. The leaves are, however, larger, fleshier and more vividly coloured. Botanically the main difference is in the well developed corolla tubes of the zebrina.

Zebrina pendula is the best-known of the house plant species. The leaves are almost metallic in appearance, the silver stripes being responsible for this. These stripes alternate with purple laid on green and the underside of the leaves is darker, ranging from mauve to purple. The leaves are usually between one and two inches long, but with good cultivation can be even longer. The stems are upright in a young plant, but will grow long and pendulous, which makes the zebrina an excellent plant for setting in a high position, with the trails hanging downwards. Stems should be pinched out before they grow too long lest they become straggly and weak.

A variety of pendula has been named *quadricolor*, because white, pink, purple and silver are all to be found vividly on the top surface of the leaves, with various tints and shades of purple on the undersides. Both *Z. pendula* and the quadricolor variety will sometimes produce clusters of little pink-purple flowers during the summer months. These are comparatively insignificant.

The only other species normally seen is *Z. purpusii*, which is a little larger and has thicker stems. The leaves are a purple-pink and do not have the characteristic silver stripe of pendula. Purpusii is a little more delicate than pendula.

Zebrinas will root as easily as tradescantias, and when they are pinched out to prevent them becoming too straggly it is a good thing to push the nipped-off ends into the soil of the pot, where they will quickly grow. Light is necessary to help the zebrinas to keep their colour, and again it is helpful to keep them slightly on the dry side.

3

FLOWERING PLANTS

The plants described in this chapter are grown not so much for their foliage as for their flowers. As flowers are ephemeral, the plants are never particularly attractive without them, and as a general rule flowering plants must be regarded as temporary decoration. This does not necessarily mean that the plants will last only a short time, but rather that their decorative period is shorter than that of foliage plants.

Many flowering plants can be removed from our living-rooms after their flowers have finished and placed in the greenhouse or sometimes even the garden. With careful treatment many of them will produce flowers again, when they can once more be brought indoors as home decoration.

Most flowering plants like a steadily warm and humid atmosphere, and will live longer and flower over a longer period if they are kept in a greenhouse in the conditions they prefer. The fact that they are suggested for room decoration means that they can, with careful treatment, give useful service even under conditions they do not really enjoy.

Many of the plants mentioned are given or received as Christmas presents. They have been forced into flower under highly artificial conditions, and consequently their decorative life in the peak of condition is brief. Little can be done about this, but we should accept with gratitude the fact that our plant growers have sufficient skill to give us beauty and colour which we should otherwise have to do without completely at that season of the year.

Azalea Indica

This magnificent plant is generally available shortly before and after Christmas, and is always freely given and received as a present. Its flowers are generally double, and are in various tints and shades of red or white. The plants frequently come from Belgium, and are grown on to flower in British greenhouses before being placed on the market. The root ball is frequently heavily pruned and the plants are placed in small pots filled with almost pure peat. Under these highly artificial conditions it is a marvel that the plants flower at all, but in fact they do and are usually covered in gorgeous bloom when they are at their best.

No azalea grown under these conditions can be expected to last for long. The actual period of decorative life can vary from a few days to several weeks, depending on conditions in the home, and great care must be taken with these plants if they are to give of their best.

The soil in the pot must always be kept moist; it must *never* be allowed to dry out. The plant must be kept in a warm position, away from all draughts, not too near a window or a radiator, and preferably out of a room which is likely to be filled with tobacco smoke or gas fumes, or which is subjected to dramatic changes of temperature. Many of our living-rooms get very warm and close during the evening, and then cool off rapidly during the night and much of the next day. The plant should not be stood in sunlight. To provide it with the necessary humidity it is helpful to give it a light spray with clean tepid water once a day, and to place the pot in moist peat or similar moisture retentive material.

When the flowers have finally gone, the plant can be

Caladium candidum—close-up of leaf

Maranta

Chlorophytum capense variegatum

Hedera helix Chicago, H. canariensis, H. helix Montgomery, H. canariensis

saved and with luck even brought to flower in the next season. It must still be kept moist at the roots but it can be given a cooler position. When spring arrives and frosts are no longer to be feared, the plant should be re-potted in a mixture of acid peat and loam. It should then be plunged complete with pot in a cool and shaded border in the garden. Even here it must not be allowed to become dry, and in times of hot dry weather the foliage should receive a light sprinkling of water once a day. Before the frosts arrive again it must be brought indoors and placed in warmth. Humidity then is of great importance, and in the absence of a greenhouse it will be essential to spray the plant lightly but regularly. A little feeding at this time will help to plump out the flower buds and give it the necessary strength to produce its profusion of bloom.

Begonia

The ornamental leaf begonias, such as *Begonia rex*, have been described in the section on foliage plants, and here we shall discuss briefly the species which provide us with flowers. There are so many of these, and their naming and division into groups is so complex and sometimes even so inaccurate, that it has been necessary to over-simplify to some extent.

In general it can be said that the easiest and most rewarding of the flowering begonias to grow as house plants are the *Semperflorens* and Gloire de Lorraine groups, both of which are fibrous rooted. Members of the former group will flower almost perpetually if kept under good conditions, throwing up clusters of red, pink, orange or white flowers. Gloire de Lorraine begonias are technically known as winter flowering because in fact they bloom during the dark and dirty days of winter, but some of them will continue in flower for almost the whole year. In our Cotswold cottage we have an old jam-making pan of bronze with a cast iron handle. It was filled a year or more ago with half a dozen Gloire de Lorraine begonias. They have flowered almost continuously ever since and have given us enormous pleasure at very little cost in cash or labour.

All the fibrous begonias like a loose, rich, well-drained soil, plenty of water during the summer months, and regular feeding while they are in flower. Semperflorens varieties like plenty of sunshine and can stand being a little drier at the roots. The Lorraine group also likes warmth but prefers a little more humidity. Both demand clean air, and we have found that our plants are always very much more successful in the country than in the town.

Brunfelsia

This delightful plant, almost perpetually covered in delicate blue scented flowers during the summer, is named after one of the first botanical artists, Otto Brunfels, a Carthusian monk of the 15th and 16th century. Once again it is not generally listed by the house plant specialists, and can only be obtained by chance or by application to greenhouse growers.

Brunfelsia calycina is the most popular species. Its delicately perfumed flowers open as purple, change to a paler tint, and become finally almost white. The flowers usually take three days to open and to die, changing colour all the time. For this reason I have heard of them being called "Yesterday, To-day and To-morrow." The flowers appear in large trusses, and individual blooms are round and flat when fully opened.

As usual with flowering plants, brunfelsia requires plenty of light. It will stand surprisingly cool conditions but some warmth gives better results. To help it along even further, and to promote a lavish display of flowers, a little pruning in the spring is useful. During the summer the roots should always be kept moist, but in winter an almost dry soil should be the rule.

The brunfelsia does not like lime, and soils should be mixed with this in view. Add plenty of peat and leaf mould, but keep the mixture open and light. Re-pot when flowering has finished and if possible give extra warmth at this time. To prolong the flowering period, keep the plant fairly cool, feed lightly with any fertiliser that does not contain lime, and give it an occasional light spray with clean tepid water.

Bulb Flowers

Whether or not bulb flowers are properly classified as house plants, there can be no question that they are often produced in the home, and so deserve a place in these pages. As methods of growing them are well known I shall merely summarise here.

Narcissi, hyacinths, and tulips are the most frequently grown bulb flowers, probably because they are easiest and least likely to cause trouble. It is also possible, however, to produce flowers from bulbs of crocuses, snowdrops and grape hyacinths, to mention only a few of the better known. The aid of a heated greenhouse is really necessary in order to flower most of the other bulbs.

Planting methods are similar for all bulb flowers which are being grown indoors. The bulb fibre or soil used must be damp but not wet, and ample drainage material must lie at the bottom of the bowl or pot used. Bulbs should be sat on a layer of fibre and then covered with more, leaving just their noses showing. The bowls should then be put away in a cold dark place to make roots. It is best to place them outdoors, but a cold dark shed will suffice. While they are making roots it is essential that they never dry out. Roots usually take about two months to form, and when the foliage is beginning to show the bowls can be brought indoors. They should not be subjected immediately to warmth and light, however, but should be put in a cool position at first, being gradually given more warmth as they become acclimatised. Only when the foliage has become a good healthy green should the plants be given normal room warmth and the light from a window. This light is apt to make the flowers and foliage turn away from the interior of the room, unless the plant is turned frequently to balance the amount of light received by every side. It is possible to buy "prepared" bulbs which have been specially treated to make them flower early. These cost a little more, but require the same treatment.

Hyacinths are particularly adapted to growing in water alone. Special hyacinth glasses are best, where the bulb is placed in the top section with its bottom just above the water. Roots will grow downwards into the water, but the bulb itself should not touch it. Most other bulb flowers will also grow in water, but in order to anchor the bulbs it is best to grow them in pebbles. However, it is necessary to make quite sure that the water does not evaporate completely, and that the bulbs are not sitting on bare stones.

Calceolaria

The gaudy, pouch-like flowers of the calceolaria are unmistakable and not, perhaps, to everyone's taste. The flowers are certainly bright, and coming as they do at the end of dreary winter, they are frequently bought as a touch of brightness and gaiety.

Although the plants are grown under fairly warm and humid conditions, they are generally toughened up before being sent to market, and when brought home should be given a place in a not too warm section of the house. They should never be placed in a window in the sun, for they do not take to too bright a light. Avoid all draughts and give as much humidity as can be obtained without actually spraying the plants. Because of the masses of bloom on these plants when they are at their peak, it is helpful to feed them quite generously during their flowering period, as this will help them remain in bloom for a longer time.

Cineraria

The daisy-like cineraria, blue, purple, red, pink or white, is a hybrid or variety of *Senecio cruentus*. It cannot be kept for long in the home, but modern varieties are so gay, so floriferous and so inexpensive that they have achieved a great popularity, and many thousands are sold each year.

Never try to keep cinerarias indoors if you like to live in close, centrally-heated rooms. They need plenty of air, without being in draughts, and plenty of light. They grow quickly and therefore need to be watered frequently. The roots should always be kept moist. Once the plants have finished flowering they should be thrown away, for there is little that can be done for them. In any case they are inexpensive enough to be used for purely temporary decoration.

Cobaea

Strictly a garden plant, the *Cobaea scandens*, or "Cup and Saucer Plant," can be grown quite easily indoors as long as it is given plenty of light. The popular name indicates the shape of the flower, which is a large greenish-whitish-purplish cup standing in the centre of a still larger saucer. If the plant is well grown some of the flowers will be fertilised, and will produce in the autumn a large fruit or seed pod swelling from the centre of the flower. It is a climbing vine which grows with extreme rapidity and will quickly cover a wall. It needs some support, but its tendrils will catch hold of trellis work or string and pull the growing shoots upwards.

Although normally grown as an annual, a cobaea will sometimes survive a winter, even out of doors. As the foliage is apt to look a little miserable in the winter, however, it is no credit to home decoration and it is much better to grow it annually from seed. This should be fresh, and preferably sown in some heat in a good rich open soil.

The cobaea is named after Father B. Cobo, a Jesuit missionary who went to Mexico in the 17th century, and, fascinated with the flora around him, became a passionate naturalist.

Cyclamen

Of the hundreds of thousands of cyclamen bought each year at Christmas time, probably ninety per cent die prematurely through neglect and lack of understanding of their needs. They may not be easy to keep from year to year, but there is no question that it can be done—and without the necessity of a greenhouse.

The florist cyclamen is *C. persicum*, but there are many varieties and hybrids on the market. Probably the best of these is the comparatively recently introduced *Decora* strain, which came originally from Belgium. This has two easily recognised characteristics: the flowers and flower buds rising vertically from the centre of the plant, and the heart-shaped silver markings on the leaves. The foliage of the Decora strain of cyclamen is in many ways as lovely as the flowers themselves, and has been enthusiastically adopted by many florists for use in decorations and even in bouquets. This strain is also tougher than some of the others.

Watering is the clue to the successful keeping of cyclamen plants for long periods. In the first place the plant should never be allowed to become dry. The roots should be kept constantly moist. Secondly, the corm from which the flowers and foliage grow rests on the top of the soil, and water should never be allowed to collect on its surface, otherwise stem rot is likely to set in and the plant will die. The best way to water cyclamen is from the base. In fact water is so important that this is one of the rare plants which can actually be stood in a little puddle of water. It is not advisable to do this for long periods, but if the flower pot is stood in a saucer which has a little water poured into it whenever it is dry, this water will soon be absorbed by the pot. It is even safer to stand the pot on gravel which is kept constantly moist, or to plunge it in moist peat.

Cyclamen do not like to live in hot stuffy rooms, and always do better for longer periods in parts of the house which are not constantly lived in and so kept too hot or too filled with tobacco smoke. They like plenty of light.

When each flower fades the stem should be grasped firmly and plucked from the corm. It should come away quite cleanly. This will help existing buds to break into bloom and induce the formation of further flower buds.

When the flowers have finished and the leaves turn yellow, watering should gradually be reduced until the plant is kept almost dry. When all danger of frost is past the pot should be plunged in a shaded and sheltered border in the garden. Re-pot the plant in August, being careful to leave half the corm showing above the soil. Bring the plant indoors and gradually increase the amount of water you give it. If it is in garden soil, give it light feeds of balanced fertiliser, but if John Innes soil is used this is not necessary. It should begin to flower again during the winter.

Erica

The heaths or heather sold in florist shops, usually at Christmas time, come mainly from South Africa. The best known is *Erica hyemalis*, but some British heathers are sometimes used. They are difficult to keep indoors for long periods, for they quickly shed their flowers and their tiny leaves. They are inexpensive, however, and so can be treated as temporary plants. It is unlikely that they can be kept from year to year without the special treatment that necessitates a heated greenhouse.

The ericas are planted in tiny pots in peat and sand. They like to have their roots constantly moist but not wet, and because of their calcifuge nature hate any water containing lime. Even tap water does not suit them, and rain water should always be used to keep them moist. They should be kept cool, away from all forms of heating, and out of all draughts.

Fuchsia

I must confess to a great love for the fuchsia, and its delicate, frilly, feminine flowers. We grow a number of them in our garden in the country and less often we have them indoors. There are tremendous numbers of species and varieties, and it is always best to go to a specialist grower for plants rather than to rely on what is obtainable from flower shops or markets.

It must be admitted that fuchsias do much better out of doors than they do in the home, but this need not deter us, for they can always be taken out into the garden after they have served us for some time indoors, and there they will continue to give us value for many years if they are properly tended. Some species are too tender for the garden and need a greenhouse, but there are others that will live for years outside with only the slightest of protection during the coldest days. In Gloucestershire we never give our plants any protection and so far we have lost none.

The plants indoors must be given a cool position. They do not mind a little shade, but should be kept clear of draughts. Roots should be kept constantly moist or buds will drop. When autumn comes the pots should gradually be dried off until they receive hardly any water for the whole of the winter. When the days begin to lengthen again in February, the plants should be pruned to shape and a little more water and a little more heat should be given. A gentle spray with clean tepid water will help them along at this stage, and doses of dilute fertiliser will plump out the flower buds. If the plants have grown vigorously they may need re-potting. Use John Innes potting soil with a little sharp sand added in order to ensure good drainage.

Hydrangea

Although the hydrangea can sometimes be rather a large plant to have indoors, it is so much loved and so spectacular in its bloom, that if you have large enough rooms it is well worth considering as a house plant. With reasonable care it can last for a very long time in rooms which are not too warm, too dry, or too subject to draughts.

Hydrangea macrophylla var. hortensis (frequently known as *H. hortensis*) is the most frequently seen variety. It produces massive and well-known blooms of pink or white where the soil is slightly alkaline or neutral, and blue where the soil is acid. The latter colour can be obtained even with alkaline soils by treating with aluminium sulphate or the new sequestrine.

The plants like to be moist at the roots, and appreciate an occasional spray over flowers and foliage. They should be kept cool and away from all draughts. Light is helpful, but not necessary, for brief periods. The normal flowering period is between late winter and late summer. After this time the plant can be plunged in the garden, pruned to shape, and brought indoors again when the frosts arrive. Rain water should always be used in preference to anything of an alkaline nature, as these plants are lovers of acid soils.

Impatiens

One of our more popular house plants, the impatiens, or "Busy Lizzie," is a balsam, and although it is sometimes found to be difficult to grow well, it is often seen in full bloom and bursting with health in the most improbable situations.

Impatiens sultani is the most frequently seen species, although *I. holstii* is also popular. Most of the species seem to come from the areas bordering the Indian Ocean. They are soft and fleshy plants with red, pink, or white flowers in various tints. They are perennials and with reasonable care can be kept in flower almost the whole year round.

In summer they grow quickly, easily, and healthily, but in winter they require more careful treatment. As might be expected from their fleshy stems they like to have plenty of water when they are growing in the summer. In winter they should be kept on the dry side. The soil should be rich, and as they are so rampant in growth they require frequent doses of weak fertiliser. This does not apply in the winter, when they should be kept warm, away from all draughts, almost dry, and in as much light as can be given away from a cold and draughty window. As it grows so quickly the plant should be pinched back occasionally to keep it bushy and pretty rather than leggy and straggly. The pinched-out shoots will root easily, even in plain water. This should be done towards the end of the summer, and the rooted cuttings should be planted out and tended carefully during the winter to give new plants in the spring and summer.

Orchid

Orchids are difficult, but they *can* be grown in the home and need not be expensive.

If we accept these three statements as true (and to the best of my knowledge they are) then it would take a whole book to examine and discuss all the possibilities. For the orchid family is a huge one, and although the greatest part of it can be ruled out as unsuitable for home culture, we should still be left with an enormous list. It is certainly my belief that there exists in the orchid family a real potential storehouse for the enthusiastic (and probably experienced) house plant grower.

Being such a large family, orchids vary tremendously, but so far as we are immediately concerned, we must divide them into the terrestrial (growing in the soil) and the epiphytic (growing on trees) species. Because most of the terrestrial orchids depend for their health on a soil fungus which infects their roots, we can rule them out. The specially prepared and sterilised soils we are more or less forced to use for house plants will not permit this fungus to live, and the plants consequently suffer.

When we turn to the epiphytic orchids we run into a further difficulty, but one which fortunately is not insurmountable. Instead of using normal soils, orchids of this type should be grown in osmunda fibre, with the addition of a little sphagnum moss. Both of these materials can be obtained from specialist growers and, in fact, it is generally better to get any necessary re-potting done by the specialist himself. There are several orchid growers and importers in and near London who will be willing to help.

Temperatures for growing orchids are of less importance

(though they must never be too low) than humidity and watering. Humidity can be achieved in the home to a certain extent by plunging pots in moist peat, but watering depends greatly on the species grown, and no hard and fast rules can be laid down.

When we come to mentioning species suitable for culture in the home we once again run into trouble, for so often we find that improved forms and hybrids are much more easily grown than some of the natural species. There are no large stocks in this country of any particular plant, and for this reason I should really content myself with advising interested readers to get in touch with a reputable orchid specialist, seek his co-operation and advice and obtain from him what varieties he recommends as most suitable. It may help, however, to mention just a few of the best known types of orchids, and to discuss very briefly their requirements for home culture. Perhaps the best known type is the *cattleya*, which is an epiphyte. It grows from a pseudo bulb which serves to a certain extent as a storage unit for both food and moisture. The roots should be allowed to dry out almost entirely between waterings, and plants should receive a daily spraying of their foliage with clean water, preferably at room temperature. They like filtered light such as they receive in their native jungles, which means that as far as we are concerned in our homes they should lie somewhere near a south window or perhaps directly in a west window. Best of all would be for them to be placed in a south window, with one or two heavily foliaged plants directly between the sun and the orchid plants themselves.

Among other epiphytic orchids are the *odontoglossums*, which appear to prefer somewhat cooler conditions than their cousins, probably because they come largely from mountain areas. They must nevertheless receive just as much humidity. A little more direct light should be given to the odonts, but never bright sunlight. When these plants come into bloom their flowers will last for months on the stem.

The slipper orchids, the popular *cypripediums*, are terrestrials and therefore difficult to grow without special growing mediums. I mentioned above that a special mould is present in the soil of most terrestrial orchids, and this is not normally available to plants grown in sterile soil. For this reason, cyps should be grown in mixtures made up from osmunda fibre, sphagnum moss, and similar non-soil materials best obtained from an orchid specialist. Cyps must have good drainage, for they do not possess the pseudo bulb which helps to nurture some other orchids. Their roots must be kept moist at all times but not actually drowned.

Oncidiums are epiphytes which require treatment similar to that demanded by cattleyas. Their long flowering spikes can be beautiful indeed.

An epiphyte which does not have a pseudo bulb is the *phalaenopsis*, perhaps one of the easier orchids for the home as long as it gets the humidity and watering it demands. It must be kept moist at all times, and a daily spraying with water will help both to provide the necessary humidity and the moisture required by the roots. Phalaenopsis likes plenty of food, and a regular feeding schedule accompanied by plenty of moisture will produce annual sprays of gorgeous flowers from this long-lived plant.

Pelargonium

At time of writing we have in our home in the country between 20 and 30 pelargoniums (geraniums) in pots. Most are small, a few are six to eight feet tall. Many are in bloom in February, and I think it will be true to say that in no month of the year are we ever without pelargonium flowers. To some experts our unorthodoxy regarding pelargoniums may be regarded as heresy. But from the foregoing it will be seen that it works.

The pelargonium is a most rewarding plant. It is easy to grow, simple to propagate, prodigal with its flowers, full of colour with or without flowers, capable of making either a bushy or a tall plant, and undemanding in time and temper. In other words it is an ideal subject for house decoration.

In general it might be said that the Regal, Fancy, Zonal and Ivy Leaved are best for culture in the home, but some of the others could well be grown satisfactorily. It might also be said that in every case it would be an advantage to have the facilities of a greenhouse to which plants could be sent for a rest and for refreshment after their duty stint in the home. This is not essential, however, for although some plants will certainly become exhausted with intensive cultivation, a few cuttings can easily be taken from them and the mother plants then discarded. There will thus be a constant flow of replacement plants.

Lavish feeding and watering in summer is the general rule, together with drier conditions in winter. Unfortunately this treatment frequently makes for lush growth of foliage and sparse bloom. Our own treatment inclines towards a starvation diet for established plants, so as to get masses of flower, and richer feeding of young plants which have fairly recently succeeded in making their roots after being struck as cuttings. Regular pinching out of spent flowers is also necessary to obtain a succession of bloom.

The orthodox time for taking cuttings is in the summer, in July or August. We take them all the year round with the exception of the coldest months of the winter. Short joints of firm stem, some four to six inches long, should be cut from the mother plant and inserted in a pot of well-drained soil which is no more than damp. While these cuttings are trying to make roots they should be kept shaded from sun and in a draught-free position. As soon as new shoots are seen to be growing, the plants can be given more water and after a week or two a gentle feed will help them along. Pinching out some of the new shoots will help to produce plants of good shape.

Some of our tall plants have been grown simply by pinching out unwanted shoots and so inducing the plants to grow upwards. A certain amount of care is needed here, for falling leaves sometimes make a bare and leggy plant. On the other hand if the plant is given normal care, it is quite possible to make a pillar of green and scarlet which stretches from floor to ceiling. The tallest plants are supported by means of long canes and are grown only in large and heavy pots which will not be upset or knocked over.

When spring arrives most of the pelargoniums go out into the garden, some in tubs and troughs, some in the flower beds. Only a few are kept indoors, mainly those that are being trained as "ceiling lifters." When they go out to the garden most plants are pruned to shape and cuttings taken to be grown on in pots indoors. These can go out again a little later in the season. Some cuttings from these prunings are also struck (with varying success it must be admitted) merely by pushing them into the soil in the flower bed.

As the days begin to get shorter and the possibility of an early frost appears, all plants are taken indoors. In some cases cuttings alone are taken and the mother plant is discarded completely. Those plants taken indoors are watered quite lavishly to begin with, and the amounts given gradually reduced until in the dead of winter the pots are kept almost dry.

Poinsettia

I hesitated about including *Euphorbia pulcherrima*, popularly known as the poinsettia, in this section devoted to flowering plants, for the flowers of the poinsettia are actually the quite insignificant pea-sized yellow bobbles in the centre of the magnificent scarlet bracts (modified leaves), which are the glory and the fame of this plant.

Unless you are very green-fingered and have a greenhouse, you must regard the poinsettia as a temporary plant, to be enjoyed for a few weeks, probably over the Christmas season, and then discarded. With some care it is possible to keep the plants until they begin quite naturally to shed their leaves, their flowering period having then been completed. It is then advisable gradually to reduce the amount of water until the plants are almost completely dry. In the spring the long main shoot should be cut back quite severely and watering should gradually begin again. Gentle feeding should begin at the same time, or if it appears necessary the plant can be re-potted, using a soil with slightly more sharp sand in it than usual. To bring them on to flower and to colour the vivid bracts some degree of heat and humidity is necessary, heat and humidity in fact which can only be obtained in a greenhouse. Once the bracts are colouring, however, the plants should be hardened off gradually before they are removed from the greenhouse and brought into the home.

Although the poinsettia is known mainly for its vivid scarlet bracts, there are varieties and hybrids with white or pink bracts. Normally, too, they are fairly tall, but some of the latest introductions are much shorter and consequently give a more concentrated splash of colour.

To keep the plants in the home make sure that they never get dry at the roots, that they never sit in draughts, that they do not occupy too warm and dry a position, that they never get a whiff of gas in the air and that they are given as humid an atmosphere as possible. Remember that the poinsettia is a bleeder, and that the poisonous white sap will flow if the bark is damaged. It will continue to flow until it is stopped artificially by singeing or by drying the cut or damaged portion with sand or some similar substance. Where it is intended to use poinsettias as cut flowers, for example in a flower arrangement, it is much more satisfactory to use the entire plant, roots and all, than to cut the stems. The roots can be knocked from the pot, washed under the tap and stood in water just as a cut flower would be.

Primula

Thousands of primulas are grown each year and sold by florists, in markets, and even by street traders at very low prices, for decoration in the home. The best varieties as a rule are *P. malacoides* and *P. obconica*, each of which with its gay flowers is too familiar to require description.

They like to be kept always moist at the roots, in a cool, well-lit position out of hot sun. They do not like polluted air, and gas fumes are quickly fatal to them. A mild dose of fertiliser while they are in flower will prolong the flowering period and keep the leaves a rich green for a longer time.

The plants can, in fact, be kept almost indefinitely after the flowers have faded, but the leaves alone do not look attractive and are not at their best after the flowers have passed. At this time the plants can be divided or re-potted, and if given a little fertiliser will eventually begin to show buds again. It is better, however, and more normal practice, to raise the plants from seed and treat them as annuals.

Saintpaulia

Known popularly as the "African Violet," this charming plant did, in fact, come originally from tropical Africa, but it is not a member of the viola family, and most of the tremendous number of varieties and hybrids do not even resemble the violet in appearance. It is named after Baron Walter von Saint Paul-Illaire, who discovered the best known species, *S. ionantha* towards the end of the nineteenth century, and it is actually a member of the *Gesneriaceae*, which family includes the gloxinia.

Saintpaulias are some of our most charming and delightful house plants, and the growth of their popularity in this country is slowed only by the difficulty of cultivating them, although I should mention that every time I say this I get into severe trouble from the many enthusiasts. They generally need higher temperatures than those which obtain in the average British home, this being substantiated by the fact that they are much more popular in the United States, where homes are kept very much warmer than they are here. They also need a considerable degree of humidity, complete freedom from draughts and gas fumes, lack of variation in temperatures, careful watering, and plenty of light.

The plants are sometimes apt to suffer from petiole rot, and we have found ourselves that using plastic instead of earthenware pots seems to help here. The tender little stems sometimes rest against the pot edge, and earthenware seems to hold concentrations of certain salts which set up this distinctive rot. The plastic surfaces cannot absorb these salts.

Saintpaulias are now available not only in their characteristic violet colour with the vivid yellow centre, but they come also in white, pink, blue and many tints and shades of these colours. They can be single flowers, semi-double and double. The foliage varies also in shape and colour, some being almost smooth, some very hairy, some being green, some almost purple. It is possible to make a very varied collection of saintpaulias.

The need of saintpaulias for controlled conditions, and in particular their need for light, is so great that some enthusiasts grow them in entirely artificial conditions. In special cases, with artificial light and heating, they will live much more happily than in the more haphazard surroundings of the average home.

Watering should be carried out very carefully, preferably from below, for spots of water on the hairy leaves can cause "burning" or brown spots on the leaves. In order to give the plants the humidity they require it is helpful to plunge the pots in a moisture retentive material, and we have found ourselves that we get excellent results by growing plants in a receptacle similar to a goldfish bowl. This lets in plenty of light but retains humidity, and generates a micro-climate of its own around the plant. The plants like a very gentle feed while they are growing well.

Saintpaulias can be propagated by several means, the safest of which is probably leaf cuttings. These leaf cuttings can actually be used several times. Some nurserymen who supply saintpaulia plants will also sell leaf cuttings, and from these it is possible to start a considerable collection.

Solanum
Bushy little plants with round or conical berries of yellow, orange, red, white or purple, the solanums are usually given or received as Christmas presents and are most frequently seen at that time of year. Because we do not see them at other seasons suggests, rightly, that they are difficult to keep.

The solanum is a species of a genus of some 900, the most important and best-known member of which is the familiar potato. So far as we are concerned there are two species generally available as house plants. They are *S. capsicastrum*, with conical berries purple, red, white or orange, and *S. pseudocapsicum*, with rounder orange or yellow berries.

Both need to be kept moist at all times but dislike a close, hot atmosphere. A daily gentle spray with clean tepid water will help retain the leaves and the berries. It is impossible to keep them in good condition without a greenhouse, and they are best treated as temporary plants.

4

CACTI AND OTHER SUCCULENTS

All cacti are succulents, but not all succulents are cacti. Succulents are distinguished by their fleshy stem or leaf tissue, and many of the cacti have evolved because of their habitat into growing organisms that have done away entirely with their leaves. The main virtue of the succulents is that by means of their fleshy bodies they have enabled themselves to live for long periods with a minimum of moisture. What they do, obviously, is to store within their swollen bodies the moisture they require for their future sustenance, and to restore themselves from the more than adequate supplies of water received during a brief rainy season.

Some cacti live in desert regions where they are subjected to intense heat during the day, with cold and heavily-dewed nights. Others live high on the slopes of mountains where they exist happily under conditions we should call cold. Temperatures are thus of differing importance to differing species. On the other hand all cacti require considerable concentrations of intense light, which gives us another clue to the way we should treat them in our homes. This is partly why they are so popular. Another reason is the ever-present hope that they can be persuaded to flower. It has been said, falsely, that a cactus flowers only once in its lifetime. In fact, there is no reason why, once you have succeeded in getting your cactus to flower, it will not continue to do so every year—but it needs coaxing.

Nearly all the cacti that we are likely to grow in our

homes and greenhouses belong to one tribe, the *cereeae*, and most of them will thrive under normal living conditions, given certain minimums of light and temperature.

The main thing to understand about cacti is that on the whole they are desert plants living in arid areas, which get much sun and torrential downpours of rain at certain concentrated periods. Temperatures are high in summer months and light is good. Cacti, however, come from as far north as Alaska, and high on the peaks of the Rocky Mountains. Many are subjected to sub-zero weather which they can stand because their roots are comparatively dry. This indicates that during the cold winter months the plants should be allowed to dry out almost completely.

Because most cacti live in sand or rock, they seldom suffer attack from the disease organisms which live in leaf mould or other humus containing material. Their resistance to fungus is slight, and soils apt to harbour fungoid spores should be avoided. Cactus soil should consist of equal parts of medium loam and coarse (really coarse) sand with the addition of a little peat. People who live in cities and consequently find loam difficult to obtain, or who seek a more accurate definition of soil mixtures, can go to the invaluable soil mixtures prepared by the John Innes Research Institute. A standard John Innes potting compost can be taken as a base, adding one-fifth by bulk of coarse sand and a further one-fifth of crushed brick. some experts recommend the addition of a tiny portion of charcoal in small pieces: this helps to keep the soil sweet.

This mixture will contain a small degree of fertiliser. Although not necessary to the cultivation of cacti, this can do no harm, and is preferable to the addition of separate and possibly less balanced fertilisers. These sometimes contain more nitrogen or green-growth-promoting substances than potash and phosphorus, which assist ripening and root growth respectively.

The root spread of a cactus is roughly equal to the area of growth above soil. If, therefore, a purchased plant is smaller than the pot containing it, it is usually safe to leave the plant in this pot until the surface diameter is larger than the pot in which it is growing, when it is advisable to re-pot it. Cramped roots are apt to starve the plant and to prevent it from flowering.

When planting cacti in new pots it is best to fill at least one third of the pot with broken flower pots, pebbles, or similar aids to drainage. On top of this should come a layer of sand, and, finally, only in the top half or so should come the soil in which the cactus is actually planted. While this soil is being sifted around the root system, the pot should be tapped vigorously on to the table or other surface in order to consolidate soil around the roots. If the soil is rammed tight with the fingers or the handle of a trowel, it is liable to pack too firmly and hinder drainage.

When a plant has been newly potted (or for that matter when a cactus plant has been newly bought) it should be placed in a good south window as near to the light as possible. If it is winter and cold, then presumably the room is heated and the plant will receive some warmth during the day, though possibly not at night. In the latter case, it should be moved slightly into the room during the hours of darkness so that it is not frosted through being too close to the glass. On the other hand, if the sun is hot and bright during the summer, one should beware of burning and give some protection against this. In winter, cacti should be kept in temperatures of no more than 40 to 50 deg. F. and watered lightly; give them enough to keep them alive and plump without starting them into growth.

As with most house plants, watering is the main problem when keeping cacti. The best method of watering is to take the entire pot to a bucket, sink, or tub, and submerge it entirely (though not the plant) until water begins to trickle over the edge. Bubbles will normally rise to the surface, and when these have finished the plant is well soaked. It should then be removed and placed on some surface where excess moisture can drain away. This process is vital, for while moisture is draining away from the hole in the base of the pot, air is being sucked in through the surface soil. This air is as important to root growth as the moisture itself.

During the winter, cacti need little beyond a light watering every four or five weeks. This should be gradually increased during early April until the summer, when they can be watered as frequently as twice weekly. It is important to remember, that, when they are getting hot sun for long periods, cacti need to be well watered at frequent intervals. They should not, of course, be kept damp, but should be given a good soaking whenever they dry up. From August, the watering should be gradually reduced until, after the end of September, they are kept almost dry. Plenty of hot sun in summer with cool, dry soil conditions in winter will frequently produce annual flowering.

Spring is the critical time for encouraging cacti to bloom. After a winter's rest the flower buds begin to form, and if the plant is given too much water at this time there will be a tendency for it to make green growth rather than flowers. Just enough water should be given to enable the buds to develop, and only when it is obvious that they are well on their way should more generous amounts of water be applied; otherwise they will sometimes dry up.

When the flowers actually appear on the cacti plant, watering should be really lavish and quite unlike normal cactus watering. In fact, with some varieties it might be advisable to stand the pots in a little saucer of water, to make quite sure that they are getting enough moisture during the period they are in flower. Weak feeding with diluted liquid fertiliser can also be helpful in getting the plant over this period of strain.

With reasonable care, pests and diseases give little trouble to cacti. Over-watering, or watering in little dribbles so that only the top section of the soil is moist, will sometimes result in root rot. This can be recognised if the plant rocks on its foundations or appears to be loose in the pot. If the plant is knocked from its pot it will be found that many of the roots have turned brown or have even rotted completely away. The action demanded is a good root pruning with a pair of scissors and re-potting in fresh soil. New roots will quickly develop. Perhaps the base of the plant may also be damaged in cases of root rot, or other damage to the plant tissue may be seen. Cacti respond well to surgery, and if the damaged portion is cut away with a razor blade or sharp knife the wound will quickly heal.

Mealy bug, scale and red spider sometimes attack cacti, particularly if they are grown near other plants. A spray with a white oil emulsion will clear this trouble. Most house plant and cactus growers swear by "Volck," a white oil mixture that looks almost like paint and must be diluted. It is obtainable from most good garden stores and those Boots branches that do not stock it can obtain it for you.

When handling cacti gloves should always be worn. The spines easily penetrate the flesh and are hard to remove. If a portion of spine is in the flesh and cannot be seen or removed with tweezers, a piece of transparent adhesive tape pressed over the spot and then torn away will usually carry the tiny piece with it.

Cacti can look delightful in dish or bowl gardens, but beware! Always make quite sure that all the residents of the bowl have the same water requirements. It is no use planting water-loving plants with cacti, for one or the other will suffer.

Ten easy plants
(Easy to get, easy to grow)

Aspidistra	Philodendron
Chlorophytum	Platycerium
Cissus	Sansevieria
Fatshedera	Saxifraga
Hedera	Tradescantia

Ten colourful house plants

Aechmea	Codiaeum (Croton)
Anthurium	Cryptanthus
Aphelandra	Dieffenbachia
Begonia rex	Dracaena
Calathea	Saintpaulia

Six that will grow really large

Fatshedera	Monstera
Ficus	Philodendron
Hedera	Tetrastigma

Six climbers or scramblers

Cissus	Rhoicissus
Hedera	Saxifraga
Plectranthus	Tradescantia

GLOSSARY

Aerial root. Any root which appears on a stem above soil level.

Aroid. Any plant of the family Araceae, notably anthurium, monstera, philodendron, syngonium.

Axil. The point where a leaf or leaf stalk (petiole) joins the main stem.

Bract. A modified leaf at the base of a flower stem, notably the scarlet, pink or white bracts of the poinsettia.

Bromeliad. A member of the family Bromeliaceae, notably aechmea, billbergia, cryptanthus.

Calcifuge. Any plant which dislikes lime or chalk in the soil.

Corm. A root storage organ of thickened stem rather than scales as with a bulb.

Corolla. The inner whorl or leaves or petals of a flower.

Cultivar. A cultivated rather than natural variety.

Epiphyte. A non-parasitic plant which grows on another plant, notably some orchids and some bromeliads.

Florapak. A spongy foamed urea formaldehyde used mainly as a stem holder for flower arrangement which absorbs and holds moisture. Obtainable from florists' shops.

Glochid. The barbed bristle or spine seen on so many cacti.

Monoecious. A plant bearing flowers of both sexes.

Offset. A baby plant produced beside another and easily separated.

Osmunda fibre. The dried, matted, fibrous roots of osmunda fern. Obtained from horticultural sundriesmen and specialist nurseries.

Petiole. A leaf stalk.

Rhizome. An underground, rooted stem producing shoots at intervals.

Roots. Although all plants are fed and anchored by their roots these can vary widely. They can take the form of a bulb, a corm or a tuber, all of which are food storage organs, or they can be fibrous, thong- or string-like.

Scape. A flower stem bearing no leaves such as that of the amaryllis.

Sepal. One of the leaves which together form tne calyx of a flower.

Spadix. A flower spike with a fleshy stem. Usually protected by a spathe.

Spathe. A leaf or bract surrounding or enclosing a spadix.

Sphagnum moss. A particularly spongy type of bog moss which absorbs water readily and is therefore useful as a packing material.

Stolon. Or runner; a shoot which runs along the soil surface and produces roots at the end or intermediately.

Stomata. Pores on the leaves of plants.

Tendril. Modified leaflets, leaves or shoots produced by many vines and other climbers and used as a means of climbing or clinging to any convenient support.

Vermiculite. An expanded mineral, very light in weight which will absorb and hold many times its own weight in water, hence a good growing and packing medium. It is completely sterile. Obtainable from garden stores.

INDEX OF ILLUSTRATIONS

Index

125